HOURS OF OPPORTUNITY

VOLUME 1

Lessons from Five Cities on Building Systems to Improve After-School, Summer School, and Other Out-of-School-Time Programs

SUSAN J. **BODILLY** JENNIFER SLOAN **MCCOMBS** NATE **ORR**
ETHAN **SCHERER** LOUAY **CONSTANT** DANIEL **GERSHWIN**

T0159308

Commissioned by

The **Wallace** Foundation

Supporting ideas.
Sharing solutions.
Expanding opportunities.

RAND EDUCATION

The research in this report was produced within RAND Education, a unit of the RAND Corporation. The research was commissioned by The Wallace Foundation.

Library of Congress Cataloging-in-Publication Data

Hours of opportunity / Susan J. Bodilly.
    v. cm.
    Includes bibliographical references and index.
    Contents: v. 1. Lessons from five cities on building systems to improve after-school, summer school, and other out-of-school-time programs
    ISBN 978-0-8330-5048-9 (v. 1) -- ISBN 978-0-8330-5049-6 (v. 2)
        1. After-school programs—United States—Case studies. 2. Summer school—United States—Case studies. 3. School improvement programs—United States—Case studies. I. Bodilly, Susan J.

    LC34.4.H68 2010
    371.8—dc22

                                                                    2010031804

The RAND Corporation is a nonprofit institution that helps improve policy and decisionmaking through research and analysis. RAND's publications do not necessarily reflect the opinions of its research clients and sponsors.

RAND® is a registered trademark.

Cover design by Pete Soriano

© Copyright 2010 RAND Corporation

Published 2010 by the RAND Corporation
1776 Main Street, P.O. Box 2138, Santa Monica, CA 90407-2138
1200 South Hayes Street, Arlington, VA 22202-5050
4570 Fifth Avenue, Suite 600, Pittsburgh, PA 15213-2665
RAND URL: http://www.rand.org/
To order RAND documents or to obtain additional information, contact
Distribution Services: Telephone: (310) 451-7002;
Fax: (310) 451-6915; Email: order@rand.org

Preface

High-quality out-of-school-time (OST) programs, which for the purposes here include after-school and summer programs, have the potential to help children and youth succeed and develop to their fullest potential. However, the OST systems that provide such programs in U.S. cities still suffer from fragmentation and lack of coordination. The result is often poor access and poor quality for those most in need of these services. In an effort to spur the creation of citywide systems of high-quality OST programs, The Wallace Foundation established an out-of-school learning initiative to fund OST system-building efforts in five cities: Boston, Chicago, New York City, Providence, and Washington, D.C. All the sites were established with the following goals:

- Increase access to and participation in OST programs.
- Improve the quality of OST programs.
- Build an information, technology, and communication infrastructure to facilitate better management and support for OST programs.
- Work toward sustaining OST programs and the systems designed to support them.

In January 2008, The Wallace Foundation asked the RAND Corporation to document the progress of these cities toward their goals and to examine the development and use of management information systems to track participation. This monograph outlines the data and methods used in the analysis, the cities' early planning efforts, and each site's progress toward improved access and quality, use of information systems, and greater sustainment. It concludes with a discussion of the factors that enabled coordinated system-building efforts and lessons for other cities. Two companion publications, *Hours of Opportunity, Volume 2: The Power of Data to Improve After-School Programs Citywide* (McCombs, Orr, et al., 2010) and *Hours of Opportunity, Volume 3: Profiles of Five Cities Improving After-School Programs Through a Systems Approach* (McCombs, Bodilly, et al., 2010), focus on Wallace-funded cities' use of management information systems and present detailed case studies, respectively. The findings of the study should be of interest to policymakers and practitioners involved in improving OST services, especially at the city level.

This research was conducted by RAND Education, a unit of the RAND Corporation.

The research sponsor, The Wallace Foundation, seeks to support and share effective ideas and practices to improve learning and enrichment opportunities for children. Its current objectives are to improve the quality of schools, primarily by developing and placing effective principals in high-need schools; improve the quality of and access to out-of-school-time programs through coordinated city systems and by strengthening the financial management skills of providers; integrate in- and out-of-school learning by supporting efforts to reimagine and expand learning time during the traditional school day and year as well as during the summer months, helping expand access to arts learning, and using technology as a tool for teaching and promoting creativity and imagination. For more information and research on these and related topics, please visit The Wallace Foundation Knowledge Center at www.wallacefoundation.org.

Contents

Tables

Summary

High-quality out-of-school-time (OST) programs, which for our purposes include both after-school and summer learning programs, have been shown to positively affect youth development and reduce negative behaviors. At the same time, the provision of OST programming in urban centers has been criticized for poor quality and lack of access for those most in need of services. In response, The Wallace Foundation sponsored an initiative in 2003 to help five cities develop better coordinating mechanisms to reduce OST fragmentation, redundancy, and inefficiency and to increase OST access and quality. The Wallace Foundation first provided each site with a planning grant to support the development of a business plan. After The Foundation approved a site's plan, the site received its implementation grant. The initiative began with a planning grant to Providence, Rhode Island, in 2003, followed by grants to New York City, Boston, Chicago, and Washington, D.C. The Foundation's funds were to be used for cross-agency and within-agency planning and coordination to meet the initiative's goals. In 2008, The Foundation asked RAND to assess the progress of the five sites.

Purpose of This Study

The RAND study had two interrelated parts. The first, reported here, was to describe the sites' work under the grant and to analyze the conditions and activities that contributed to their progress in building a coordinated system of services that would meet the initiative's goals:

increasing access, improving quality, developing and using information for decisionmaking, and planning for sustainability. The second part of the study, reported in *Hours of Opportunity*, Volume 2: *The Power of Data to Improve After-School Programs Citywide* (McCombs, Orr, et al., 2010), involved a detailed analysis of the cities' progress in building and implementing management information (MI) systems to track student enrollment and attendance, including—but not limited to—The Wallace Foundation grantees. In this monograph, we specifically answer the following research questions:

1. What decisions did the sites make about approaches to improving OST systems during the early phases of the initiative? What drove these decisions?
2. What progress did sites make toward increasing access, improving quality, using data-based decisionmaking, and improving sustainability?
3. How did collaboration and coordination enable progress? What other enablers were important?

The analysis provides interesting examples of what Wallace grantees did and why, as well as the proximate result—the immediate effect on OST provision, structure, access, quality assurance, and information for planning and sustainability. In-depth case studies of the individual cities are presented in *Hours of Opportunity*, Volume 3: *Profiles of Five Cities Improving After-School Programs Through a Systems Approach* (McCombs, Bodilly, et al., 2010).

Approach

To address the research questions, we used a qualitative, replicated case-study approach in which the unit of analysis was the citywide, multiorganizational initiative funded by The Wallace Foundation. Our literature review of collaborative interagency reform efforts in the OST and other social service sectors further guided the development of our research questions, data-collection instruments, review of the literature, and interviews with key city leaders, leaders of community-based organizations, principals, providers, and staff at The Wallace Foundation. These data were developed into case studies constructed around key descriptive and analytic categories that factored in evidence from key individuals and reports about the history of the OST sector in that site. We then conducted a cross-site analysis to identify patterns of activities that led to greater coordination across agencies and organizations. To further guide other cities in their improvement efforts, we examined and include examples of the types of activities that the five cities used in their attempts to improve service provision. The study did not measure the effects of these efforts on students and families.

Findings

Variation in Starting Conditions Among the Sites
The Wallace Foundation chose five cities, each with its own context, demographics, and organizational characteristics that influenced the development and implementation of the initiative. The variation afforded the opportunity to examine coordination and system building in multiple contexts, highlighting both city-specific and shared factors that appeared to contribute to or inhibit progress.

The sites varied in size. New York City had more than 8 million residents, while Providence had approximately 175,000. Each city had a high-need student population, with more than 60 percent of students eligible under federal guidelines for free or reduced-price lunch. Sites varied in their start dates. Providence began its planning grant early in 2003, followed by New York City later that year; the three other sites started in 2005. The sites varied in their existing infrastructure for OST provision. For example, the city of Providence did not contribute strongly to after-school programming prior to the grant, while the city governments in New York City and Chicago provided significant funding across an array of city agencies.

Early Efforts

The Wallace Foundation provided planning grants to sites to encourage them to develop concrete ideas, with the expectation that solid plans would lead to implementation grants. It encouraged sites to use market research, needs assessments, and other information-gathering and analysis methods to identify specific targets for their work. The market research and gap analyses proved to be crucial starting points for several cities: This work identified areas of the city without provision, age groups that lacked accessible programs, and issues of concern to parents and students that acted as barriers to participation. Plans were developed to target these specific issues.

The different histories and structures of the cities led to different coordination structures. New York City and Chicago were led by city agencies and concentrated on improving services funded by the city. In Boston, Washington, D.C., and Providence, intermediaries led the work initially.

What Was Attempted and Progress Toward Goals

The Foundation set four broad goals for the sites. We tracked the specific activities that the sites undertook in each of these broad areas through the spring of 2009. While we do not describe all of these activities in detail in this monograph, we do provide several examples of what the sites tried to accomplish.

Goal 1: Increase Access and Participation. Providence, New York City, Washington, D.C., and Boston focused on access and addressed issues related to convenience and lack of access by opening additional programs in underserved neighborhoods and schools and, in one site, by providing transportation. Many sites also developed online program locators that parents and students could use to identify programming in their local area. These methods of improving access, combined with greater funding, increased the number of program locations and slots available to students in four of the five cities (Boston, Washington, D.C., New York City, and Providence).

Goal 2: Improve Quality. All five sites focused some energy on improving quality of programming. The mechanisms used varied but included the development and widespread use of quality standards, quality-assessment systems for providers, and incentives and contractual mechanisms to encourage improvement. Several sites offered professional development programs for OST providers and the coordinators who managed OST programming in schools.

Goal 3: Develop Information Systems for Decisionmaking. All the cities devoted considerable energy to developing web-based MI systems to track enrollment, attendance, and demographic data. These systems also collected information about providers and their programs. Data from these systems were used to determine which programs were attracting students, and, for the first time, cities were able to make use of data for planning. Interviewees reported that analytic capability was limited in some sites but that the data-based decisionmaking and communication strategies improved the agencies' ability to plan. In addition, Washington D.C., New York City, and Providence reported using data from these systems to produce the evidence needed to argue for greater funding based on both need and improved effectiveness.

Goal 4: Plan for Financial Sustainability. Under the grant, the cities were asked to plan and develop sustainable funding strategies. While some cities had diversified funding sources, all sites were struggling with issues of financial sustainment when the study ended, exacerbated by the downturn in the national economy.

Collaboration and Other Enablers of Coordinated System Building

The cities varied in their use of mechanisms for collaboration, and this affected their progress. New York City and Providence, the sites with more longevity, used collaborative approaches to make significant progress toward the larger goal of a more coordinated system. In its first 18 months, Chicago concentrated its effort almost exclusively on the development of MI systems to enable further collaboration in building a better OST system. Boston struggled with collaboration in the early years of the initiative, which impeded its progress in creating a more coordinated system. Washington, D.C., simultaneously encouraged collaboration through a city-level coordinating structure while the school district pushed forward with a major initiative mostly on its own. Interviewees in all sites noted that there was still more work to be done in this regard.

The sites used a variety of collaborative mechanisms, including data collection and analysis to identify gaps in provision; consolidating functions within specific agencies; establishing a coordination structure, such as a steering committee, to ensure regular meetings; vesting a special adviser with the power and authority to ensure interagency cooperation; establishing memoranda of understanding (MOUs) across agencies to document specific agreements on the sharing of resources and interpretation of policy; creating structures for cross-agency information sharing used in joint decisionmaking; and providing incentives and supports for coordination.

The adept use of these and other mechanisms by some sites inspired a shared vision among the collaborators, which paid off significantly in the later years of the initiative. And, clearly, the funding provided by The Wallace Foundation acted as a catalyst for collaboration.

Mayors and their representatives proved to be crucial enablers of collaboration and system building. Actions by mayors, including restructuring agencies, increasing funding in the city budget, and demanding progress reports, positively affected the efforts. A recession, with its related drop in city and state budgets, was under way by the end of the study, and it significantly challenged the cities' efforts to expand access, in particular.

Themes for Other Cities

The findings of the study suggest some themes that other cities working to improve OST provision might consider as they move forward.

Coordinated system-building efforts can improve access and quality. Four of the five sites successfully increased the number of students served. At the end of the study, all of them were in the process of building quality-assessment systems to help identify poorly performing providers and offer training and incentives for improvement. Four of the cities were using newly developed information to improve decisions regarding access and quality. However, all were struggling with the financial sustainment goal. Thus, The Wallace Foundation investment provided some proof that city organizations could work in a cooperative fashion to promote better OST services and programming.

Each city has a unique context that should drive goals. Based on their unique conditions, each city selected a slightly different focus, such as a targeted age group, targeted locations, or an emphasis on quality versus access. Other cities considering how to improve provision should not simply adopt one of these specific approaches, but should examine their own circumstances to identify how to best propel their efforts forward.

Investments in early planning and management information system development paid off. The sites deliberately considered the specific assets in place, the organizations involved, the challenges faced, and the funding available, which helped them identify targets for improvements. Collaborative early planning efforts also supported shared goals among the organizations and agencies that later proved useful as the efforts unfolded and inevitably faced challenges. By collectively going through early planning processes, organizations at sites such as Providence and New York City had the ability to effectively face challenges together. Sites that did not stress the development of shared goals, especially Boston, did not fare as well in meeting their OST goals. In addition, early collaboration on needs assessments paved the way in several instances for the cooperation needed to develop an MI system that provided the data necessary to further improve access and quality. Collection and analysis of data focused on specific improvements, allowed the sites to assess whether progress was being made, and supported arguments for additional funding. In addition, shared data enabled some sites to maintain their shared goals across organizations. New York City and Providence, with more years of experience, had pushed farther than the other sites in this direction by the end of the study.

Cities can consider an array of approaches to improving access and quality. The study sites adopted an array of ways to improve access and quality. Improving access involved identifying underserved populations and using appropriate mechanisms to increase enrollment, such as placement of programs in neighborhood schools, providing transportation to and from the programs, and providing programs at no cost to participants. Each city addressed quality through the adoption of standards, the use of the standards to assess program quality, provision of professional development, and evaluation of their efforts.

Cities can consider an array of mechanisms to increase coordination. The sites used an array of collaborative mechanisms to improve coordination—including restructuring, consolidating roles, establishing coordinating committees or steering committees, appointing mayoral envoys to ensure interagency cooperation, developing interagency MOUs, sharing information, and changing rules and incentives. Putting such mechanisms in place ensured that some sites kept moving forward toward shared goals.

Several enablers were important. Interviewees agreed on several important enablers of collaborative efforts: building a common vision among stakeholders, an early assessment of needs, development of an MI system, an actively supportive mayor, the buy-in of schools, and investment funding. The major constraint on progress cited was lack of funding and stovepiped funding that prohibited integrated services. Most sites rated the mayor's support as essential, and, in three sites, mayoral involvement went beyond simple encouragement or "bully pulpit" statements. Active mayors crucially supported efforts in their cities by restructuring the organizational landscape, realigning funding sources, creating special adviser positions to ensure cooperation across agencies, chairing forums and overseeing intermediaries, and demanding analysis of outcomes for consideration in funding decisions. Rather than waiting for such mayors to emerge, it might be possible for other cities to educate their mayor early in the process about how he or she can positively participate in such an initiative.

Thus, other cities should consider what actions they can take within the confines of their specific environment. Small steps forward can add up over time to significant improvements for underserved children. This document provides important ideas and concepts to help inform those considerations.

Acknowledgments

Many individuals contributed to this study, which was made possible by the interest and support of the sponsor, The Wallace Foundation. In particular, we thank Zakia Redd, Ann Stone, and Ed Pauly from The Foundation's evaluation team; Nancy Devine, Sheila Murphy, and Dara Rose from the communities team; and Pam Mendenal and Lucas Held from the communication team. All provided important feedback that improved the content of this monograph.

We are particularly grateful for the cooperation and support provided by each of the cities in the study—Boston, Chicago, New York City, Providence, and Washington, D.C. Our respondents' willingness to share their successes and challenges in this area will aid other cities in their efforts to improve OST program provision. Reviews by city agency and intermediary staff also improved the accuracy and presentation of this monograph. We are indebted to all the individuals who participated in the study and shared their valuable time and insights with us.

We appreciate the insightful reviews and comments provided by Heather Weiss and our RAND colleague Catherine Augustine. The clarity of this monograph benefited greatly from their comments and suggestions.

Finally, we thank our colleague Dahlia Lichter for organizing our site visits and helping to keep the project on track.

Abbreviations

BCYF	Boston Centers for Youth and Families
BOSTnet	Build the Out-of-School Time Network
CBO	community-based organization
CLI	Community Learning Initiative
DCPS	District of Columbia Public Schools
DELTAS	Boston Public Schools Department of Extended Learning Time, Afterschool, and Services
DYCD	New York City Department of Youth and Community Development
FY	fiscal year
ICSIC	Interagency Collaboration and Services Integration Commission
MI	management information
MOU	memorandum of understanding
NYSAN	New York State Afterschool Network
OST	out-of-school time
PASA	Providence After School Alliance
PASE	Partnership for After School Education

PSS	Partners for Student Success
RFP	request for proposals
RIPQA	Rhode Island Program Quality Assessment

CHAPTER ONE

Introduction

Youth (grades kindergarten through 12) across the United States participate in publicly supported out-of-school-time (OST) programs in group settings after school and in summertime. Such programs include simple after-school care services to support working parents, programs specifically structured to help reduce problem behaviors, programs that reinforce academic achievement, and programs that offer access to sports, arts, crafts, and other activities. Local service providers may be a combination of community-based organizations (CBOs), city agencies, and intermediary organizations. The collection of OST providers and funders in a city can often be fragmented and uncoordinated, however (Bodilly and Beckett, 2005; Halpern, 2006).

Recent studies indicate that high-quality, well-managed and -structured OST opportunities can help youth develop critical academic, social, and emotional attributes and skills, especially if offered consistently and persistently over time (Lauer et al., 2006; Bodilly and Beckett, 2005). This research has drawn attention to whether publicly supported programs meet these conditions and whether they are effective avenues for youth development. In particular, cities are attempting to improve the access and quality of programs to ensure that more youth have the opportunity to achieve the results associated with the most effective programs.

Foundation Goals and Expectations

To further promote effective provision, The Wallace Foundation decided to fund an out-of-school-time learning initiative to help five cities (Providence, New York City, Boston, Chicago, and Washington, D.C.) develop and test ways to plan and implement coordinated OST programming that, ideally, would achieve four goals: increased access, improved quality, better use of data for decisionmaking, and increased sustainability.

Increased Access to and Participation in OST Programs. The Foundation expected sites to ascertain the demand for services from different age groups, how to increase demand among certain groups, and the most effective locations in which to meet demand with supply in order to develop plans to improve participation. To increase access, the sites could more systematically address such issues as safety (in transit and at the program location), access to transportation, affordability, and convenience (hours of operation amenable to children's and parents' schedules). They could build program locator systems or otherwise work to ensure that parents and children knew about the programs and how to access them. In addition, cities could conduct marketing activities to appeal to underparticipating groups, such as teens. Finally, the cities could open more slots at more locations to increase enrollment.

Improved Quality of OST Programs. While high-quality OST programs can produce positive outcomes for participating students, the quality of programming within a city is typically mixed. The Foundation expected sites to create mechanisms to support high-quality programs and ensure strong enrollment, attendance, and desired student outcomes. Activities could involve developing standards, using standards to assess program quality, monitoring improvement over time, and vetting providers upon entry into the field with common criteria. Performance incentives could be offered to programs. In addition, the cities had to ensure that a supply of professional providers was available to meet expansion and quality goals simultaneously, implying that some professional development and training might be needed.

Finally, sites could undertake evaluations of the effort to ensure that the changes resulted in improved outcomes.

Better Use of Information Systems for Improved Decision-making. Cities have not traditionally invested in developing data systems to support improvements. As a result, many cities across the United States are unable to accurately report the enrollment and participation of youth in OST programs. To support access and quality, cities needed to track program activities and monitor participation and attendance rates. This required the adoption of management information (MI) systems to track programs and participation, if they did not already exist.

Improved Financial Sustainability. Finally, The Foundation was interested in making a large investment in system-building efforts, but not in funding the OST programs themselves or becoming a perpetual donor. Thus, grantees were required to develop sustainable funding sources for OST programming and system-building activities.

Site-Level Goals. While the four goals drove the efforts, The Foundation understood that sites would have to apply them in accordance with their own specific circumstances and city needs; therefore, each site was to develop its own methods for meeting those goals. For example, a site might concentrate on improving access for a specific group of children—middle school teens, for example. It might already have a fully developed MI system; therefore, it would concentrate elsewhere or devote resources to one activity in the early years and focus on others in later years.

Purpose of This Monograph

To share the learning from this initiative with the larger OST field, The Wallace Foundation asked RAND to document the five cities' progress toward building the systems infrastructure to provide more coordinated and effective services. The purpose of the RAND study, conducted between January 2008 and May 2009, was to examine how the participating cities were developing and aligning local assets to maximize collective effectiveness in delivering sustained, high-quality

OST programming to school-age children. In our analysis, we focused
on the many differences across the sites to provide insights into how
grantees made important choices.

This examination had two tasks: (1) an analytic description of
the development of the five OST sites supported by the grant, addressing what the sites attempted to do under the grant and the progress
they made, and (2) a description of the MI systems established to track
student participation in each of the Wallace-funded sites as well as in
other cities. This monograph focuses on the first task and addresses the
following questions:

1.   What decisions did the sites make about approaches to improv-
     ing OST systems during the early phases of the initiative? What
     drove these decisions?
2.   What progress did sites make toward increasing access, improv-
     ing quality, using data-based decisionmaking, and improving
     sustainability?
3.   How did collaboration and coordination enable progress? What
     other enablers were important?

The analysis provides interesting examples of what the grantees
did and the proximate result—the immediate effect on OST provision
structure, access, quality-assurance processes, information for planning, and sustainability.

Methods

Our unit of analysis was the multiorganizational initiative in each
city. We chose a replicated qualitative case-study design to answer our
research questions. The study resulted in a descriptive analysis of the
activities that the sites undertook and the conditions that led to progress toward each city's specific goals (under the broader Wallace Foundation goals). The analysis involved examining the data for similarities
and differences among the sites and extracting themes in terms of what
enabled and hindered progress. We exploited the variation among the

sites in context, conditions, and what was attempted to provide useful comparisons about the ways in which different choices influenced progress toward coordination and system building. These variations are covered in Chapter Two. The examples should help other cities better plan improvements in their OST infrastructure.

In this section, we present the findings from the literature reviews that guided our investigation, data sources for the research questions, and the analytic approach. We reviewed the literature on efforts to build greater coordination across public service agencies to help determine the types of mechanisms that the sites might use to promote system building, and we used this information to develop protocols and guide our analysis. We used the sites' own proposals and plans to determine what their systems looked like before the grant and what they intended to accomplish, which we compared to what they had accomplished by the spring of 2009. The descriptions of the grant's goals acted as the categories that we tracked and guided our search for themes in the efforts that promoted progress.

Themes from the Literature on Coordination and Collaboration Across Agencies

A review of the literature indicated that the sites would likely face challenges as they attempted to develop citywide approaches in which multiple organizations were at work.[1] These organizations might include government agencies, schools, CBOs, foundations, state and federal oversight agencies, and agencies with funding streams that target children. (See Bodilly and Becket, 2005, for a more detailed description of the actors involved in OST provision.)

In general, coordination of organizations in the public sector is undertaken to achieve a shared goal that is considered important to each organization but often not achievable individually due to a lack of political power or resources. In sectors characterized by resource constraints, such as public OST provision, coordinated approaches also

---

[1] We condensed findings from the following sources: Bodilly, Chun, et al., 2004; Bodilly and Beckett, 2005; Bodilly, Augustine, and Zakaras, 2008; Dluhy, 1990; Banathy and Jenlink, 2004; Hall and Harvey, 2002; Halpern, Sielberger, and Robb, 2001; Halpern, 2006; Keith, 1993; Mattressich and Monsey, 1992; Russell et al., 2006; and Tushnet, 1993.

hold the promise of increasing the efficiency of provision by reducing duplication and gaps in service. This increased efficiency can translate into expanded access. Furthermore, agreement among organizations as to what constitutes quality provision can result in more consistent quality across programs. However, these theoretical benefits are gained only through intense and sustained efforts at multiorganizational coordination or system building.

The literature on public-sector interagency coordination or collaboration to improve systems indicates that these types of efforts are slow to develop, fragile, typically struggle to sustain themselves over time, and develop differently in each site due to the heavy influence of city contextual factors. Past research has identified specific barriers and enablers to such multiorganizational coordination efforts. Factors influencing the success of initiatives include leadership capability, sufficient and capable staffing, buy-in from major stakeholders, public support, communication among stakeholders, funding, and the city context. In particular, past efforts have depended heavily on the emergence of legitimate initiative leaders who use unifying techniques to ensure buy-in and harmony among participating organizations and key managers.

The literature describes a series of activities in which sites might engage to varying degrees, which we used to develop our approach to data collection and to present our findings.

Conduct a needs and assets assessment. A starting point might be the identification of gaps in services and system weaknesses, along with community assets that can be leveraged to address gaps. Such data can be gathered through market research, discussions with stakeholders, and audits.

Build shared goals. Development of and buy-in for a shared set of goals is the foundation on which all activities depend. The group of agencies or organizations should work toward a commonly held series of goals or expected performance improvements, perhaps through meetings, regular communication, and sharing of information to build common understanding and purpose.

Consolidate or develop more coordinated structures and roles. To promote efficiency and clarity in the system, the effort might involve reorganizing agencies into more effective or efficient structures with clear roles and the oversight needed to move forward.

Coordinate among groups. Routine and effective communication and coordination among organizations is needed to facilitate joint work or group decisionmaking and may be accomplished through regular meetings among representatives or a coordinating organization.

Plan for and implement coordinated activities. The organizations might develop plans for joint or complementary activities to increase impact. Fundraising and resource redistribution might be key components of the effort.

Develop, analyze, and share information. Collaborative activities, like any improvement efforts, usually involve the development, analysis, and sharing of information. In this particular instance, that might include collecting and using data on access to and participation in programs, developing and using assessment tools to evaluate learning and diagnose and address failure, assessing the effectiveness of staff training and professional development, and collecting and using data to find funding flows and determine where additional resources are needed. MI systems provide information for these improvement efforts; analytic talent and dedicated time are also required to interpret and make use of the data collected. Defined reporting structures also encourage consistent sharing of information.

Communicate with the public or engage stakeholders. Coordination initiatives often involve the development and communication of information about the state of the field and what could be done to improve it, ensuring that this information flows to the public to garner increased partners and support in the effort. Public relations and advocacy campaigns help gain support among parents, policymakers, and community leaders by making visible the need and articulating the possible solutions. In addition, agencies must develop the means to communicate with the public about the services being provided to ensure usage. This is especially true for after-school programs with historically low rates of attendance.

Establish incentives, rules, and supports. To ensure that the efforts continue cities must put in place quality standards and evaluations of programs against standards and provide supports, such as professional development, to help providers meet those standards. They might also provide clear incentives for improvement or take punitive action if providers fail to meet standards or expectations.

Data Sources

Our primary goal was to track and describe what the sites did and how they did it. We could not observe progress as it was made; the study began well after the sites had started their work, and intensive observations across sites were beyond the resources of the study. To understand where sites started and what their intentions were (research question 1), we reviewed statements made in initial proposals and business plans concerning each of the four expectation categories: improving access, improving quality, developing MI systems, and developing and implementing plans for financial sustainability. We also collected background information from primary sources.

To determine the sites' progress (research question 2), we collected data on activities during the grant period and records of accomplishment. A significant portion of the data came from the annual reports and business plans submitted by the sites to The Wallace Foundation, along with reports from market surveys and other data-collection efforts. The other primary source of data was interviews at the five sites and with staff at The Wallace Foundation. We conducted two rounds of interviews, the first in spring 2008 and the second in spring 2009. In the interviews, we asked about (1) the general conditions of OST at the sites at the beginning of the grant period and what the sites hoped to accomplish with the grant; (2) activities conducted during the planning phase and how they informed future efforts; (3) their progress toward the four categories of expectations; (4) how they used cooperation, coordination, or collaboration to accomplish their tasks and whether it was important to the effort; and (5) what enabled or impeded their efforts and why.

Table 1.1 shows the number of interviewees by type at each of the sites. We interviewed 125 individuals in total. Note that the table counts each interviewee once. In many cases, we interviewed these contacts twice over the course of the study. At each site, we aimed to interview key individuals who were involved with the initiative during

Table 1.1
Number of Interviews, by Site and Affiliation

Affiliation	Providence	New York City	Boston	Chicago	Washington, D.C.
Mayor's office	2	2	1	0	4
City/state agencies	3	9	4	10	1
District and school	5	2	8	4	5
Intermediary	9	4	7	0	8
Providers	15	7	4	7	4
Local funders	2	3	0	0	3
Other	2	3	5	8	1
Total	38	30	29	29	26

the planning and implementation periods, including key city officials, school district officials, staff from intermediary organizations, OST providers, and foundation funders.

At some sites, a large number of people were involved, while other sites had fewer people engaged in the process. In initial interviews with Wallace Foundation staff, we asked for the names of their main points of contact and key players in the initiative at each site. We then used phone interviews to contact these actors to determine whom they thought we should interview. We also used documents such as business plans to identify who had been involved in the site's efforts over time. We contacted these individuals. We ensured that we interviewed the major players in the initiative and additional actors whom they recommended we talk with, including those in the provider community and administrators of school programs.

For each interview, RAND researchers took notes, which were supplemented by and checked against audio recordings of the interviews. Using the interview data, business plans, and progress reports submitted to The Wallace Foundation, we developed site-specific case studies, which can be found in *Hours of Opportunity*, Volume 3: *Profiles of Five Cities Improving After-School Programs Through a Systems Approach* (McCombs, Bodilly, et al., 2010). In developing the case studies, we took care to examine interviewees' responses for consistency across individuals and also looked for consistency with documents submitted to The Wallace Foundation. Cases in which there was disagreement among respondents were noted and explored in follow-up interviews. Where there were clearly divergent views, we present both views or note the uncertainty surrounding the exact events.

Analysis

We analyzed the case-study data for cross-site similarities and differences concerning the progress made toward the four goals and whether and how coordination or collaboration was useful to that progress. Variation among the sites provided us with the means to draw contrasts to help determine the conditions under which certain approaches were chosen and the conditions under which they flourished. In addition, we reviewed the interviews for examples of how one set of activities might have influenced the progress of another set; for example, the development of an MI system to track participation led to other activities, such as an effort to argue effectively for funding.

To address research question 1, we simply condensed material from the sites' proposals and our interviews to outline what each site wanted to accomplish, but we also used the coordination mechanisms listed earlier to organize the findings around key activities in the early phases, such as needs assessments and market research.

To assess the progress and how the sites accomplished it (research question 2), we took the information from the case studies and business plans and summarized it under the four goal categories.

We conducted a similar exercise on the coordination mechanisms used and how the respondents described them (research question 3). We relied on the site interviews for information about how they approached coordination and then placed that information into categories developed from the literature: conducting a needs assessment; building shared goals through meetings and ensuring regular communication and information sharing; consolidating organizations into more coordinated structures; coordinating among groups through regular meetings or the work of special committees or task forces; planning and implementing joint activities; developing, analyzing, and sharing information; communicating with the public; and providing incentives, rules, and support for improvements.

Finally, we reviewed the case studies for common enablers and constraints, allowing us to draw out themes.

The final findings were briefed to The Wallace Foundation, and each site was provided with its case study for comment. Later, the sites and The Foundation were provided with a copy of the draft report for review to ensure that our findings were factually correct as of spring 2009.

Study Caveats

This monograph offers important information about cities' efforts to build and strengthen OST systems that provide youth with access to high-quality OST programming and suggests a set of lessons learned for other cities interested in improving their OST programs. It relies on reports from our interviewees—the actual actors involved in the initiative. While we attempt to corroborate their reports by looking for consistency with other interviewees and documents, the data are perceptual and, in some cases, retrospective, which may lead to an incomplete or unintentionally biased report of events.

Each site started with little data; therefore, we cannot quantitatively describe certain changes from before the initiative to after (e.g., participation rates of enrollees). However, we can describe how the cities developed such data where none existed before. Thus, the outcomes of note are the improvements made to the cities' infrastructure that could logically connect to the initiative's goals.

This monograph covers only the accomplishments from the beginning of the grant to spring 2009. However, in each city, work has continued and activities have evolved beyond what is presented here.

Organization of This Monograph

The remainder of this monograph is organized as follows. Chapter Two describes early planning efforts in the five sites. Chapter Three details what the sites did to address the four goals. Chapter Four reviews findings about the mechanisms for coordination that were used by the sites and the factors that enabled or constrained the sites' efforts. The final chapter reflects lessons learned from these cities that could inform other cities' efforts to improve their OST systems.

CHAPTER TWO

The Early Phases of the Initiative and Decisions Made: The Importance of Context

This chapter addresses research question 1 concerning what happened in the early phases of the initiative. We found that the sites showed significant variation even before the initiative, and these differences shaped their respective goals and plans. While they had common overarching goals that aligned with The Wallace Foundation's intentions, they adapted those goals to suit their city's needs. When city context changed, it affected how the effort proceeded. The findings of the cross-case analysis point to multiple ways in which other cities can approach improving OST provision, depending on their circumstances.

First, we present further background on the steps that The Wallace Foundation took to select sites and initiate planning. Next, we describe how various aspects of city context shaped the focus and scope of the sites' initiatives. We then outline the coordinating structures developed and discuss what site respondents identified as the single most important enabler during their planning activities—the role of the mayor. We conclude by summarizing what we learned across the sites about the early planning period.

This chapter draws heavily on each grantee's planning-year proposal, business plans submitted to The Wallace Foundation, market survey reports and evaluator documents, and interviews with those at the sites involved during this formative period.

The Start of the Initiative

After deciding that it would focus a major new initiative on improving OST systems, The Wallace Foundation conducted its own investigation to find promising sites in 2002. It identified three cities, and Providence stood out because its new mayor was a major supporter of OST improvement with the ability to provide the necessary political backing for the initiative. After many conversations with the mayor and a major nonprofit, Rhode Island Kids Count, in the spring of 2003, The Foundation gave Providence a one-year business planning grant to determine how to best use the funding. It encouraged Providence to use a consultant and a market research firm to understand the needs, interests, and concerns of students and parents. The Foundation approved the business plan and awarded Providence a five-year implementation grant in 2004 (see Table 2.1).

The Wallace Foundation soon began having conversations with representatives in New York City, having been impressed with the mayor's commitment to OST expansion, dedication to data analysis, and willingness to restructure the city's government. In the fall of 2003, The Foundation gave New York City a one-year planning grant to determine gaps in services and what parents wanted in terms of

Table 2.1
Planning Date, Implementation Date, and Funding Amount

Site	Planning Grant Dates	Implementation Grant Dates	Implementation Grant Funding Amount
Providence	April 2003– April 2004	June 2004– June 2009	$5 million over 5 years
New York City	November 2003– April 2005	April 2005– March 2010	$12 million over 5 years
Boston	October 2005– March 2006	May 2006– June 2009	$8 million over 3 years
Chicago	October 2005– March 2006	June 2006– June 2009	$8 million over 3 years
Washington, D.C.	October 2005– March 2006	April 2006– June 2009	$8 million over 3 years

programming and to gather input from key stakeholders. New York City was awarded a five-year implementation grant in spring 2005. In the fall of that year, as both Providence and New York City moved into the implementation phase with some signs of success, The Foundation approached other cities and selected Boston, Chicago, and Washington, D.C., to begin planning grants. These grants were shortened to six months, and The Foundation awarded three-year, $8 million implementation grants to these cities in the spring of 2006.

City Context and the Planning Process

The sites varied in several obvious ways at the start of the initiative, including demographics, shape of the OST sector, and unmet needs. These variations worked in tandem to shape the scope and focus of The Wallace Foundation initiative in each site.

Demographics

Table 2.2 provides demographic information from the sites at the time they were selected for the grant. The size of the cities varied substantially: New York City is about twice the size of Chicago and more than 50 times the size of Providence, the smallest city involved. What did not differ among the cities was the significant percentage of low-achieving students being served and each city's desire and need to improve OST provision.

Needs

During the planning year, the sites worked to identify strengths and weaknesses to guide the focus on the initiative.

Common Overarching Concerns. While interviewees in all the cities thought OST programs could benefit children and youth, they noted concerns about the quality of current OST programming and the potential lack of access to programming for many young people. Leaders of after-school programs in each city thought that high-quality programming could help improve behavioral and academic outcomes for children and youth by providing them with a chance to

Table 2.2
Demographics of the Cities

Demographic Characteristic	Providence (2003)	New York City (2003)	Boston (2005)	Chicago (2005)	Washington, D.C. (2005)
Population	175,878	8,125,497	596,638	2,836,800	582,049
Youth population (under 18)	27%	24%	21%	26%	22%
Median household income	$34,202	$39,937	$42,562	$41,015	$47,221
Individual poverty rate	29%	19%	22%	21%	19%
Public K–12 enrollment	27,900	1,023,674	57,349	420,982	59,616
Percentage of students eligible for free or reduced-price lunch	74%	71%	73%	74%	61%

NOTE: For a more detailed assessment and sources for the figures, see McCombs, Bodilly, et al., 2010.

engage in meaningful activities between the hours of 3:00 and 6:00 p.m. Interviewees at each site expressed concern about dropout rates, teenage crime and violence, poor school attendance, and high teenage pregnancy rates. Interviewees in police departments were particularly supportive of increasing access for older children to "keep them off the streets and productively occupied," so that they were not victims of crimes and did not engage in criminal activity. Test scores appeared to be less of a concern than the more significant negative life impacts of dropping out or incarceration, with the exception of Boston, where leaders expressed concerns about the academic achievement of students in the city's lowest-performing schools. In addition, OST programs were considered a support for working families.

Information-Gathering Efforts. The Wallace Foundation strongly encouraged the cities to undertake some type of market research or gap analysis with the planning grant funds to understand what issues were keeping children from enrolling and subsequently attending programs. It even offered the services of a company to help with the market research. Cities varied in their responses to this encouragement and in what they found when they undertook these exercises, especially as they defined gaps in coverage or weaknesses in existing programs.

Market analysis proved to be a key input to planning decisions in Providence, Washington, D.C., and New York City. These sites relied on formal surveys administered by outside consultants to parents and/ or children to clarify why children did or did not attend programs and what might attract more children to programs. New York City also used geographic information system mapping of existing programs overlaid on maps of at-risk youth populations to identify areas of unmet need. Boston and Chicago did not engage in market analysis until after the planning grant had concluded.

According to respondents and our own review of the market research documents, parents in Providence and Washington, D.C., were particularly concerned about their children's safety at the program and in transit. In addition, when compared to elementary school children, middle school and high school youths had less interest in after-school programs, often engaging instead in duties at home or work. The surveys allowed the cities to approximate the number of children who were not being served but who might attend and to understand the challenges they faced in increasing enrollment and participation.

Several cities also compared where programs were being offered to where in-need populations were concentrated. In particular, New York City's data collection and analysis showed that programs were located in areas that once had significant populations of in-need children. However, as the populations in the city shifted, new or different areas lacked programming to meet demand. Mapping student populations against program locations showed that growth in high-need populations occurred in areas not well served by existing programs. This led policymakers in New York City to push strongly to relocate programs or encourage new providers to operate in these underserved parts of the city.

Some cities identified underserved age groups. In the cases of Washington, D.C., and Providence, this seemed to be especially the case for middle school children. Those cities' market research and mapping exercises showed significant elementary school provision supported by federal funding streams that ended when children turned 12 but little provision for middle school children. In both places, school-based provision increased as the children reached high school, with more team sports, music programs, and other school-based activities.

In the three cities where this analysis took place as part of the planning process, leaders reported using the findings to shape the strategic focus of the initiative. In addition, they reported that the exercise helped fuel an appetite for more data collection, thereby contributing to support for the initiative goal of building and using better data in the OST sector.

In addition to the market research and early analysis, leaders in Providence and New York City solicited input from the public to identify needs and worked toward agreement on goals and strategies. In both cases, these processes were supported or led by the mayor's office and kicked off by the mayor himself. Interviewees in both cities commented on the value of understanding the needs and desires of providers and key OST-sector participants. In addition, they noted that this process helped gain buy-in for the initiative that continued during the implementation phase. The three other sites did not undertake stakeholder engagement efforts that were as formal or as extensive during the planning phase, perhaps due to their shorter planning grant period.

City Context and the Strategic Focus and Scope of the Initiative

City context drove the agency selected as the lead for the initiative's activities, and a combination of city context and identified need shaped the scope and focus of each city's initiative (see Table 2.3). In cities in which an agency provided significant funding for OST, a city agency was designated as the lead. In cities with a low level of city funding for OST, an intermediary took on the lead role. Initiatives led by cities tended to adopt a broader scope, while those led by intermediaries were more likely to start with a demonstration that would later be scaled after proven success.

Table 2.3
City Context, Lead, Focus, and Goals of the Planned Initiative

Site	Size	Major Sources of Funding	Identified Lead	Identified Area of Need	Focus	Goal
Providence	Small	No city funding; reliance on federal, state, and philanthropic sources	Providence After School Alliance	Lack of options for middle school students; safety and transportation concerns	Middle school students	Expand slots for high-quality programming to middle school students
New York City	Very large	City a major funder; much of city funds for at-risk youth concentrated in Department of Youth and Community Development (DYCD)	DYCD	Underserved areas and populations; inefficient supply	New York City youth, particularly high-need populations	Improve efficiency of all DYCD-funded OST programs; increase scale
Boston	Mid-sized	Dispersed; mixed public and private	Boston Beyond	Persistently low-performing schools	Students in low-performing schools	Demonstrate Partners for Student Success full-service model in 15 low-performing schools
Chicago	Large	Multiple city agencies; After School Matters	Department of Children and Youth Services (now Family and Support Services), in coordination with other agencies	Lack of data systems, common language, and measures of program quality across multiple agencies; lack of coordinated state funding; low participation among teens	MI systems for all agencies; teens	Improve efficiency in contracting in major agencies and organizations; increase enrollment of teens
Washington, D.C.	Mid-sized	Dispersed; private and public	DC Children and Youth Investment Trust Corporation	Lack of options for middle school students; transportation	Middle school students	Demonstrate model in 5 middle schools

Providence. The city had no agencies that provided or funded OST, or even an agency dedicated to youth development, prior to this initiative. Furthermore, there was no external, intermediary organization that focused on OST programs for youth. There were, however, dozens of CBOs offering programs to small numbers of students across age groups, and CBOs operated several nationally recognized high school programs. Because there was no city agency or organization focused on OST, Rhode Island Kids Count, a statewide nonprofit, helped coordinate the planning process, which engaged all stakeholders in significant fact-based review of what existed and what was most needed.

The major task for the city was to determine who would lead the improvement efforts. The planning year resulted in the creation of an intermediary agency called Providence After School Alliance (PASA), which was the recipient of the implementation grant. Heads of several city agencies, such as the police department and the Providence Public Schools, sat on its steering committee (and later its board), which was chaired by the mayor. Given the identified need for middle school programming, the grant was to be used to create neighborhood campuses, called AfterZones, to provide middle school youth with after-school activities at their schools as well as community locations. Each AfterZone was overseen by a coordinator and several site-based staff. The intermediary was to develop an MI system to track students during program hours, develop and implement quality standards and a self-assessment tool for providers, obtain sustained funding, and ensure access for all middle school children who wanted services.

New York City. New York City had a sprawling array of providers under a large number of city agencies that did little to coordinate with each other. Two very active intermediaries that received city funding: The After-School Corporation and Partnership for After School Education (PASE). The mayor, who was a strong advocate for better, more efficient government and a supporter of better youth programming, began an initiative to improve after-school services through better use of management systems and forced interagency coordination. The city's interest was in improving the effectiveness and efficiency of the vast number of community-based providers with which it contracted for services.

In the year prior to and during the planning grant period, the city took several important steps. A city-led review of city-contracted provision for at-risk youth led to the consolidation of many programs and funds into the DYCD. Prior to this consolidation, the mayor had appointed a new commissioner of the department with a strong background in after-school services. To ensure further coordination across the many city agencies, he appointed a special adviser with fully delegated mayoral power to increase the coordination across agencies.

The mayor's special adviser and leadership from DYCD led the planning process to efficiently increase access. As part of this process, they used market research to identify underserved locations; thus, they focused the implementation grant on getting better programs across all age levels in high-need areas of the city. They developed a new contract process for providers to encourage more programs in needy areas and to promote quality by providing free professional development to OST providers. They also adopted additional strategies to increase access, including improved coordination with the schools and providing additional information to the public to encourage enrollment. All interviewees familiar with this initial effort emphasized the important role played by the mayor's special adviser in ensuring the cooperation of other agencies, regular and productive meetings, and the creation of specific memoranda of understanding (MOUs) to document agreements made among the agencies.

Boston. Several years before the Wallace grant, the mayor opened the schools until 6:00 p.m. for CBOs to provide programs to students in those schools. The mayor had backed major OST initiatives (as had major philanthropists in the city) and supported an intermediary, Build the Out-of-School Time Network (BOSTnet), which published an annual guide to OST programming. In 2004, two major, mayor-led initiatives were combined into an intermediary public-private venture called Boston After School and Beyond (Boston Beyond). Its mission was to promote OST programs through communication, data collection, research and analysis, strategic initiatives, and resource development. At the time of the planning grant phase, the OST field in Boston included the two intermediary organizations, BOSTnet and Boston Beyond, and the city provided funding primarily through the community centers operated by the Boston Centers for Youth and Families (BCYF). Boston Beyond led the planning grant because of its potential for leadership in the sector and the participation of the mayor and other key city leaders on its board.

In the planning period, the actors focused on using the grant to implement an existing initiative of the Boston Public Schools called Partners for Student Success (PSS). This initiative focused on a group of low-performing elementary schools and was intended to offer a full-service model of supports, including significantly increased after-school programming, to turn performance around. The Boston implementation proposal aligned the PSS school reforms and the after-school reforms into a single comprehensive model. The plan called for PSS to be piloted in five schools in the first year, then expanded to five additional schools in each subsequent year of the Wallace grant (15 schools total). The initiative included school-, program-, and system-level strategies. The school-level strategy included a manager of extended learning services, who would be located in each of the 15 schools to coordinate the school-level effort. The program-level strategy called for offering professional development to providers to strengthen services. At the system level, the goal was to institutionalize the PSS approach within the city and the school system. A coordinated information and evaluation system was to support the initiative. The implementation grant was given to the fledgling Boston Beyond, with the mayor's support, to implement the model by helping coordinate the work of the manager of extended learning services, offering professional development for providers to improve their services, and building a coordinated information system.

Chicago. The city had sprawling OST provision and a very highly regarded, nationally recognized, high school OST organization, After School Matters. In 2003, the mayor consolidated 50 city social service programs into the Department of Children and Youth Services, making it a major city funder of CBOs providing OST programs. This still left very large portions of OST provision under the purview of several other agencies, including the Chicago Public Schools, the Chicago

Park District, and Chicago Public Library. All these agencies funded or provided OST programming to youth; however, none of these agencies had OST provision as its sole or primary mission. The mayor's wife, chair of After School Matters, along with that organization's director, led the planning grant process, which used a steering committee structure that included the major OST organizations as well as the Chapin Hall Center for Children at the University of Chicago.

In Chicago, the grant was awarded to the city to improve coordination across the various city agencies and, especially, to fund projects that the agencies would not otherwise fund. The city's plan outlined five strategies: build and implement MI systems to track OST programs and participation that would be provided to all OST partners and providers, develop and implement a communication plan to target teens, disseminate best practices across providers, pilot a consistent way to measure and ensure OST quality, and develop strategies for long-term sustainment. While After School Matters received the grant, the effort was housed in the Department of Children and Youth Services (which later became Family and Support Services), with a multiagency coordinating committee established to coordinate the grant activities. Early activities focused on developing an MI system for each major OST funding agency. The hope was that, by working together on this endeavor, they would begin to find ways to cooperate on the other significant improvements, particularly programming for teens, who appeared to be underserved compared to elementary-level children.

Washington, D.C. In Washington, D.C., the DC Children and Youth Investment Trust Corporation (the Trust), a public-private venture founded in 1999, acted as an intermediary between city agencies and CBO providers and advocated for improved funding and programming. In addition, many city agencies provided services to youth, including the Family Court, the Department of Human Services, the Department of Corrections, the Department of Health, the Department of Parks and Recreation, the D.C. Public Library, and the Metropolitan Police Department. The Trust led the planning process in Washington, D.C.

The lack of programming for and participation among middle school youth, which was identified through market research, led the

Trust to propose the creation of high-quality OST programming in five middle schools with on-site coordinators to demonstrate what better coordination and alignment might accomplish. The model would be scaled to other middle schools after the demonstration period. The supporting infrastructure for the citywide system would have three prongs: an MI system to track enrollment and attendance, a system for using and improving standards through training, and a communication strategy. In the long term, the plan called for sustainment through absorption into the city budget.

Changes in City Context and Changes in the Structure of the Initiative

In two of the cities, the context shifted, which led to a shift in the structure and focus of the initiative.

Boston. Boston After School and Beyond received the Wallace grant and ran the program for the first two years. During this period, the organization faced a number of staffing changes, including the resignation of its executive director. Further, there were many leadership changes in various city agencies—the superintendent, the head of the Department of Health and Human Services, and the police commissioner, all of whom were ex-officio members of the Boston Beyond board. All of these aspects delayed implementation progress. In fact, the PSS demonstration occurred in only ten schools rather than the 15 planned demonstration schools. We were told by many interviewees that the relationship between Boston Beyond leadership and the mayor became strained, leading many observers we interviewed to believe that the mayor lacked confidence in the effort. In addition, there was a lack of coordination and outreach to other players in the city, perhaps in part due to the organization's staff turnover during this period. Interviewees outside of the PSS initiative did not understand how it was propelling progress toward system-building goals.

In spring 2008, The Wallace Foundation asked Boston to resubmit an implementation plan. In response to The Foundation's concerns, which were apparently shared by some of the leadership throughout the city, Boston developed a new business plan that included the active participation of the mayor's office, the superintendent's office, the Department of Extended Learning Time, Afterschool, and Services (DELTAS, a small agency within the Boston Public Schools), Boston Beyond, and other key city agencies. Interviewees described all stakeholders as engaged, active participants in the development of the new plan. Respondents thought that the process would help reinvigorate the grant and set it up for success. The new business plan placed the PSS sites into the DELTAS Triumph Collaborative, a group of Boston public schools that shared an OST model that was similar to the PSS model, including a full-time on-site coordinator supported by DELTAS. Thus, during the 2008–2009 school year, the work under the grant expanded to include all Triumph Collaborative schools (42 schools in total, including the PSS schools). The DELTAS office assumed operational responsibility for implementing the initiative. The goal of the initiative was to create lessons learned across all the sites that could then be exported to other Boston public schools to bridge the divide between school and after-school programs.

At the time of our final visit, Boston Beyond was under new leadership and in the process of reshaping its strategic focus and place within the OST community. Interviewees were hopeful about the organization's future role in the city, and the mayor's office was supportive and enthusiastic about the new leader.

In addition, interviewees described a new effort by the mayor, the Community Learning Initiative (CLI), which was led by the city agency that ran the community centers (BCYF) and was intended to bring together community centers, schools, and libraries to coordinate and expand OST learning opportunities for youth. Thus, as of spring 2009, three organizations were coordinating OST efforts in Boston (Boston Beyond, DELTAS, and BCYF); it was unclear which organization was leading system-building efforts, and all were involved in the CLI's work.

Washington, D.C. The plan for implementation was for the DC Children and Youth Investment Trust Corporation to help build local CBO capacity and to develop programming in middle schools, which would be managed by a coordinator at each middle school site. Implementation began but was soon thrown into uncertainty with a change of administration in the city.

At the beginning of the implementation grant, in the early days of the new administration, the city council passed legislation that brought the schools under mayoral control and established the Interagency Collaboration and Services Integration Commission (ICSIC). The Trust and other government agencies were asked to sit on this commission and to collaboratively plan and coordinate OST provision and other youth services for the city. This legislation moved the focus of coordinated activity away from the intermediary and toward more centralized governmental planning through ICSIC.

Finally, in the last year of the grant, and as a result of ICSIC's decisions, the District of Columbia Public Schools (DCPS) undertook a concerted and unprecedented effort to improve OST provision in the city's public schools. Taking the model developed by the Trust under the grant, DCPS moved to open the schools to CBOs during after-school hours, began the process of vetting the CBOs, and placed coordinators in each school building to work with the CBOs, principals, teachers, and parents to improve services. The school-based coordinator model developed by the Trust was implemented across the district.

Coordinating Structures

The sites took different approaches to coordinating their efforts, based on their local context. One approach concentrated on intra-agency coordination within the city, and the other relied on an intermediary organization for such coordination (see Table 2.4). In two cases, the site lead for the initiative shifted over the implementation grant period due to changes in local context.

Because the funding for OST in Chicago and New York City was concentrated in city agencies, it is logical that a city agency would assume the lead for the initiative. However, in Chicago, multiple city agencies were involved in OST, leading them toward an interagency collaborative approach. In the other cities, a key city funder of OST programs did not exist, and an intermediary agency that had the mayor's support was selected to lead the initiative.

Table 2.4
System Coordination Structures

Characteristic	Providence	New York City	Boston	Chicago	Washington, D.C.
Lead agency	Intermediary (PASA)	City agency (DYCD)	Intermediary (Boston Beyond), with school district (DELTAS)	City agency (Family and Support Services)	Intermediary (the Trust) transitioned to ICSIC
Coordinating structures	PASA board AfterZone coordinating councils	Single government agency supported by mayor's special adviser Interagency Coordinating Council of Youth as forum for discussions	Transitioned to mayor's subcabinet meeting	Cross-government agency committees	Transitioned to cross-government agency committee
Partners	PASA board includes representatives from education, police, health, parks, etc.; has 100+ community partners	Agencies representing schools, health, child care, libraries, parks, and community partners, etc.	Boston Beyond Mayor's office Agencies representing education, health, and libraries	After School Matters, Chicago Park District, Chicago Public Library, Chicago Public Schools	21 agencies serving children, including schools, health, mental health, libraries, police, etc.
Regular meetings	Regular meetings of PASA board with attendance from agency heads and mayor Monthly meetings of coordinating councils for each AfterZone	Regular meetings of Interagency Coordinating Council of Youth and other advisory boards; informal meetings as needed	Shifts over time By 2009, regular monthly meeting includes mayor's Education, Health, and Human Services Sub-Cabinet; PSS committee	Meetings of Leadership Committee, Partners for Advancing OST, Executive Committee, Pillar Committee	Regular ICSIC meetings held by mayor to address OST provision

Both Washington, D.C., and Boston began a model that had an intermediary acting as the coordinator. In Washington, D.C., the Trust was the lead coordinator prior to the new administration; however, as the new mayor and the city's public schools (which were under mayoral control) became more engaged in the work of the initiative, the locus of control for the system-building activities shifted to the city.

In Boston, the approach in place at the end of spring 2009 makes it difficult to place it in either category. As a result of the second business plan, submitted to The Wallace Foundation in the spring of 2008, PPS was incorporated in DELTAS during the 2008–2009 school year. The plan was to broaden the impact of PSS beyond the ten pilot sites to the Triumph Collaborative, coordinated by DELTAS. Boston Beyond retained overall responsibility for the PSS grant and continued to focus its attention on systemic efforts, including resource development, supporting the creation of common outcomes for OST, systemic data collection and analysis, and advocacy. In addition, by 2009, the CLI had been established and was being led by a city agency (BCYF). In spring 2009, many organizations were involved in leading efforts to improve OST program provision in Boston.

In general, partners were engaged due to interest in providing OST opportunities to youth. The grantees involved multiple partners in the work of coordinating through existing structures (e.g., New York City's Interagency Coordinating Council of Youth) or newly developed ones (e.g., Washington's Interagency Collaboration and Services Integration Commission, formed by the mayor's office to ensure coordination of services for youth). Boston's initial effort was largely confined to the demonstration schools; however, in later years, OST issues were being addressed by the mayor's Education, Health, and Human Services Sub-Cabinet, which coordinates various city agencies.

Second, no matter the organizational structure, if the partners did not meet, it would be difficult to achieve any coordination. These meetings differed based on site context. In Washington, D.C., ICSIC meetings were monthly, formal, and top-down; they were held by the mayor, and all agencies attended and presented information to him. In contrast, Chicago's partnership was driven by the goodwill of various agencies that collaborated with each other, and it established many committees that reported meeting with varying frequency, including a high-level committee led by the mayor's wife and a committee of mid-level agency leaders who were charged with implementation.

The Role of the Mayor

The previous section described how city context shaped the plans and organization of the initiative. But what our interviewees emphasized above all was the importance of mayoral actions in these early efforts. Besides the normal bully pulpit that all the mayors in these cities used, several interviewees pointed to very specific actions that influenced the outcomes of early and later efforts.

For example, the mayor of New York City made after-school provision part of his reelection platform, mentioning it in speeches and appearances. He launched the effort in a citywide summit. He restructured agencies and funding streams to ensure that it was given priority. He appointed a special adviser, who reported to him directly, to coordinate efforts among the relevant agencies and create a strategy to improve OST provision. The mayor granted the special adviser powers to work with the agencies to develop and implement a series of MOUs. For example, MOUs were used to allow the schools to stay open for CBOs, to ensure that the CBOs did not have to pay for facilities or utilities at the schools, and to ensure the health department provided proper (but not overzealous) oversight. Since the beginning of the grant, this position of mayoral adviser with the power to ensure cooperation has been funded through The Wallace Foundation grant, and interviewees regarded it as essential to the development of the effort.

Similar supportive steps were taken by the mayor of Providence, who led the effort to place the early planning effort with a well known child-advocacy group, helped create the intermediary and sat on its board, actively recruited the intermediary's executive director, reviewed progress as head of the board, and actively sought funding for programs.

As discussed earlier, the mayor of Washington, D.C., supported a restructuring of the government to enable more integrated planning for youth services across agencies. As head of the ICSIC, he also demanded information on progress and required agencies and the Trust to report regularly how services were being improved.

In Chicago, while the mayor was verbally supportive, he did not act as assertively as the mayor of New York City to push the city agencies toward more serious collaboration. In Chicago, the mayor's wife led the effort to bring in The Wallace Foundation grant. While her involvement was enough to bring the different parties to the table, it was not enough to ensure the pooling of funds, joint programming, or program consolidation across the agencies involved. Chicago instead opted to achieve coordination among agencies through the indirect process of building MI systems, which was seen as a "win-win" for all involved. Respondents could not recall being asked by the mayor for progress reports or hard data on outcomes.

According to respondents in Boston, the lack of alignment between the intermediary leader and the mayor led the fledgling program to the struggle and impeded its ability to lead system-building activities. Thus, there was little coordination in the first two years.

We take from these examples that, when dealing with multiple city agencies, the mayor can and sometimes does play a strong role in ensuring greater interagency coordination. This role also appeared to apply to the creation and support of intermediaries and the demand for reports on progress. The sites' histories illustrate effective and less effective actions that can be taken to ensure coordination and show that the bully pulpit might not be enough. In this case, actions might speak louder than words.

Summary

It is clear that the sites started in very different places but had in common The Wallace Foundation's goals and a concern about the effectiveness of their after-school programs. As they proceeded through the early phases of the effort, they began to show some distinctive differences as they adapted The Foundation's goals to their particular interests and needs, but they also experienced shifts in local governance that affected how they proceeded. From this review of the early years, we can make the following observations:

- Sites noted common problems that they thought better OST programming could help alleviate, including high dropout rates, high youth crime involvement, high teen pregnancy rates, and generally poor youth development trajectories. Improving achievement scores was not a major goal for OST programs, except in Boston, even though all the sites had low-performing students.
- Early planning, which often included significant data gathering and analysis, helped leaders identify specific targets for the efforts; these targets varied across sites and were driven by context and constraints. Engaging stakeholders in discussions of the issues facing them and the city proved to be highly valued as a means of gaining future buy-in. Providence and New York City received a full year for planning and did more extensive community engagement than the three sites, which had a shorter planning period.
- Local context determined which organization would lead the initiative. Where city agencies provided significant funding for OST programming, a city agency led the initiative. In cities without this major city funding through an agency, an intermediary led the efforts.
- When the city led the initiative, the scope tended to be broader, while intermediaries were more likely to start with a demonstration that would be scaled after proven success.
- When city context changed—for example, when mayoral control shifted—the initiative changed in response.
- Mayors and their representatives were crucial to ensuring progress in the early stages of the initiative in each city. Strong mayoral actions ensured that OST improvements rose to the top of the city's agenda and that coordination, consolidation, and restructuring across agencies occurred.

CHAPTER THREE

How Sites Attempted to Improve Access, Quality, Information, and Sustainability and the Progress They Made

The sites undertook a set of activities to meet the initiative's goals: increasing access, improving quality, developing better information to improve decisionmaking, and increasing sustainability. To answer research question 2, we tracked what each city did to achieve the four goals. We begin by describing what each of the sites achieved in terms of access, quality, information, and sustainability. We then describe the types of activities undertaken to achieve results for each goal.

Results of the OST Initiative

The sites were able to accomplish much under the Wallace grant. At the point of our final data collection (spring 2009), two of the sites had completed five years of implementation (Providence and New York City), while the other three were only two years into their implementation grant. Thus, as one would expect, we see more progress in Providence and New York City toward the goals than in the other sites (see Table 3.1).

In Providence, the AfterZones offered after-school opportunities to all middle school students, and approximately 34 percent of middle school students participated—an increase from about 500 to 1,700 slots. PASA helped secure federal 21st Century Community Learning Center funds to support the AfterZones, and PASA, with direct help from the mayor, was successful in bringing in many private donations to support system building and programs. Data on participation were used in daily decisionmaking, informed planning, and helped garner

Table 3.1
Results of the Initiative

Site	No. of Years	Coverage Goals	Increase Access and Participation	Improve Quality	Collect and Use Data	Implement Sustainability Plan
					Results	
Providence	5.5	All middle school students	Middle school participation increased from 500 youth per year to approximately 1,700 students per year (34% of middle schoolers)	Standards were created and used in all AfterZones Professional development given to all OST providers	Program and participation tracked for first time Data used for decisions and securing additional funds	Created new sources of funding—21st Century funds and expanded private funding
New York City	5	All DYCD OST programs	Increased the number of slots from approximately 45,000 to more than 80,000 Entices new programs to high-need locations	Standards created and used to assess all OST programs Free professional development for all OST providers	Program and participation tracked for first time Data used for decisions and securing additional funds	Used information from data system and evaluation to lobby for increased city funding
Boston	2.5	Triumph Collaborative schools (42 total) CLI demo begun	New programming in 5 schools that did not have programs; in 2008, 927 students enrolled in after-school programs across 10 PSS sites, but unclear how many slots were created by PSS	Prior standards guide Triumph Collaborative programs Professional development and coaching given to OST schools and programs in Triumph Collaborative	Data system in development by DELTAS	No new sources or plans

Table 3.1—Continued

Site	No. of Years	Coverage Goals	Increase Access and Participation	Improve Quality	Collect and Use Data	Implement Sustainability Plan
				Results		
Chicago	2.5	All teens	Teen campaign under way to increase participation and enrollment	Pilot under way for quality-improvement process (43 sites) based on professional development and standards	New MI systems operational and used by all youth-related agencies	No new sources
Washington, D.C.	2.5	All public schools	Programs in all DCPS schools Number of schools with OST programming prior to initiative is unknown	Professional development given to site coordinators Providers vetted	MI system already used by the Trust prior to Wallace funding DCPS tracking attendance through school system database for first time Mayor requests data at ICSIC meetings to track city progress	DCPS funds OST programming in all schools

additional funding for the efforts. Building on the AfterZone success, PASA began to support system-building efforts at the high school level.

In New York City, over the course of the initiative, DYCD moved programming to high-need areas, expanded the number of slots from 45,000 to more than 80,000, and set a uniform cost model. It required all providers to enter program and participation data into an MI system. Data from this system were used to hold providers accountable for participation, signal potential quality issues, and help garner additional funding for OST. In fact, New York City's sustainment plan was to use participation and evaluation data to prove the benefits of OST programming to attract increased city funding in an increasingly competitive environment.

In Boston, the PSS demonstration was folded into the activities of the Triumph Collaborative, a group of schools with a similar model of OST provision. In addition, Boston was just starting its complementary CLI. Participation increased in the PSS schools, as five of these schools had no OST program prior to the demonstration. In 2008, 927 students were enrolled in after-school programs across the ten PSS sites. The MI system was in development and there were no changes in how OST was funded or sustained.

All the major public agencies in Chicago had functional MI systems, and, in spring 2009, data from all agencies had been merged into a single data set to allow the agencies to review data across the entire OST system. Chicago had established a quality pilot that was under way in 43 sites, and the Chicago Public Library had led an active campaign to improve teenage participation. There was no change in how OST was funded or sustained.

In spring 2009, Washington, D.C., had OST programming in all its public schools, and each school had an on-site OST coordinator, funded by the school system. The Trust continued to use its MI system to track participation, and the school system tracked OST program participation using its school MI system. The mayor called on the schools, the Trust, and other agencies to regularly report on programs and participation.

We cannot comment on whether quality improved, as our study did not track program quality outcomes. However, each of the sites had made efforts to improve the quality of OST providers, including adopting standards, observing program quality, and giving providers professional development.

Activities to Meet The Wallace Foundation's Goals

Using proposal and interview data, we categorized the activities reported by the sites into the four goal areas. It is important to remember that New York City and Providence received their grants earlier; thus, one would expect to see more activities in the implementation phase in these sites. Greater detail on site activities can be found in McCombs, Bodilly, et al. (2010).

Goal 1: Increase Access and Participation

Across the sites, a first order of business was to increase access and participation—in specific locations or for specific populations. Efforts varied, but common activity areas, as shown in Table 3.2, were to address transportation issues, increase convenience for students, increase the number of locations and available slots in the programs, increase enrollment, and ensure affordability.

Address Transportation

Adequate transportation was identified as a key issue in the sites, with the exception of New York City and Chicago. In New York City, with its very dense population and heavy reliance on public transit, students walked or used public transportation to get to and from programs. In Chicago, the focus was on teens who already used the city's public transportation independently. Thus, lack of transportation, while still possibly prohibiting access for some, was not seen as a key concern.

In other cities without convenient city public transportation routes to schools, children had to transit from the schools to the programs or from the school-based program to home. This required the running

Table 3.2
Sites' Efforts to Increase Access and Participation

Goal	Providence	New York City	Boston	Chicago	Washington, D.C.
Address transportation	Transportation to after-school programs and home provided	Public transit already available	School programs require parent pickup	Public transit already available	Public transit already available
Increase convenience	Provide middle school programs through school-based hubs	Open programs in schools and during summer and school holidays; provide programs in underserved areas; mandate that all programs are free	Placement in PSS schools convenient for some with transportation home Planning for community center provision under the CLI	No change planned	Programs established in all DCPS schools
Increase the number of locations and available slots	Expanded slots in middle schools	Programs moved to high-need areas Number of slots expanded over time	PSS sites expanded access to programs in 10 schools	No change planned	Programs established in all DCPS schools
Increase enrollment	Zone coordinators with school staff to encourage student enrollment AfterZones promoted in advertising, flyers, parent-teacher organization meetings, open houses, and fairs	Implemented a web-based program locator Implemented a marketing campaign targeted toward parents	Implemented a web-based program locator School site coordinators work to encourage student enrollment Planning to extend programs throughout the CLI	Implemented a web-based program locator Active teen marketing campaign	Implemented a web-based program locator School site coordinators work with school staff to encourage student enrollment
Ensure affordability	Free	Free	Low fee or free	Low fee or free	Low fee or free

of additional school district buses, especially on the homeward trip. In Providence, the only transportation costs incurred by PASA are to transport students from their home schools to programs that take place in off-site locations, such as at local recreation centers, Boys and Girls Clubs, or parks and museums.

In Washington, D.C., the original focus under the Trust was on programming in neighborhood middle schools, later extended to programming in all DCPS schools. DCPS buses special education students only. All other students walk or rely on public transportation. Nonetheless, parents did express concerns about their children returning from OST programs safely, and concerns were greatest during the winter when students would have to walk home in the dark. This led some middle school OST programs to operate under winter hours, so the program ended earlier. Issues of access remained when DCPS began operating programs in all public schools. As more children switched to charter schools and more traditional schools closed, the neighborhood patterns began disappearing. Planners worried that more children would feel unsafe on the return trips home if they had to cross unfamiliar neighborhoods, especially in areas where gangs were present.

Boston interviewees noted that transportation was an unsettled issue that undercut efforts to increase access. Boston public schools use an open enrollment plan in three regions for grades K–8, with open districtwide enrollment for high school students. Every school day, children in grades K–8 commute within their region to their schools of choice using district-provided transportation, while high school students take public transit. The mayor opened the schools to after-school programs in the late 1990s, but transportation home was not provided. Thus, children found their own way home from programs or relied on parents to pick them up. Because Boston focused its OST efforts on a school-based model as opposed to a neighborhood-based model, students coming from out of the neighborhood would have to find their own way home. Finding transportation home seemed to be a key to the initiative's success. Additional transportation was not provided in the planning or implementation proposals. Instead, the initial goal of PSS was to create after-school opportunities in the students' home neighborhoods through CBOs without adding more bus routes, which would accrue transportation costs.

Increase Convenience

In four of the five cities, the planners sought to increase the convenience of the programs, hopefully increasing access by moving programs closer to the children and running the programs for more hours. Providence adopted the neighborhood campus concept, with programs offered in or near the schools and running until 5:00 p.m. with transportation home.

New York City increased convenience by moving the programs closer to underserved populations. When it put out requests for proposals (RFPs) to vendors for more programs, it specified geographic areas of the city that had to be served. Providers stepped forward to deliver programs in those underserved areas, thus increasing the convenience to the children.

In Chicago, because furthering a plan depended on the development of MI systems, we did not uncover any coordinated efforts to increase convenience, aside from those that already existed. There were community centers and parks throughout the city that already offered programs, as did the schools. Thus, the planners felt that programs were already conveniently available. In some areas, population shifts had made the location of some parks and community centers less than ideal in terms of providing youth programming to high-need populations, but moving a park or a center was considered prohibitively expensive.

In Boston, the initiative initially focused on ten low-performing schools (PSS schools) in the first two years of the grant. Five of those schools had no after-school programming prior to the grant. The plan established programs in these schools that were open until 6:00 p.m. This set-up was convenient for those who had transportation home but not for those who came from other parts of the city and did not have easy access to transportation.

Increase the Number of Locations and Available Slots

Three cities (Washington, D.C., New York City, and Providence) intended to significantly increase the number of children in after-school programs. These plans were heavily dependent on placing more quality providers into specific geographic areas and obtaining additional funding. While each worked to recruit higher-quality providers, they also aimed to recruit more providers or providers who could serve more students.

For example, leaders at the Trust concluded that it would be more effective to get small to midsized providers to agree to provide more slots than to get new providers to enter the field. This required a change in how the leaders of those small provider organizations thought about and managed their operations. The initiative in Washington, D.C., called Project My Time, established the Institute for New Leaders, New Communities, designed to train and coach leaders of small provider organizations to develop the managerial capacity to expand. Attendance at the institute would guide the CBO leader through the development of a strategic plan and actual implementation. About 60 providers were targeted for this training over a two-year period.

New York City and Providence spent considerable effort obtaining additional funding to increase the number of slots available. Providence successfully sought to get external funding through grants and federal 21st Century Community Learning Center funding for some of its AfterZones and provider organizations. AfterZones increased access among middle school children to OST programs. According to estimates provided by PASA, during the 2008–2009 school year, 34 percent of enrolled public middle school students in Providence participated in a PASA program—approximately 1,700 students. PASA estimated that only 500 middle school youth participated in OST programming each year prior to the creation of the AfterZones. New York City planners used the data they had developed to demonstrate to the mayor and city council both the need for more slots and their successes in placing more children. They were able to successfully advocate for greater funding allotments against competing programs because they could show data to support their claims. They successfully increased the budget available to DYCD for these purposes from

$46.4 million in fiscal year (FY) 2006 to $116.6 million in FY 2009, thereby increasing the number of slots from approximately 45,000 to more than 80,000.

Boston also increased the number of children participating in OST programming at its PSS sites. There was no OST programming in five of the schools prior to PSS. In 2008, 927 students were enrolled in after-school programs across the ten PSS sites.

Increase Enrollment

Early planning surveys and other more general research indicated that many children and parents did not use after-school programs because they did not know about them. Thus, each of the sites undertook efforts to increase public awareness. Four sites (Boston, Chicago, Washington, D.C., and New York City) developed online "program locators" to encourage enrollment. On these websites, consumers could type in their address, zip code, or other location information and identify programs being offered in their area. In several instances, the program locator connected to the providers' website so that consumers could read descriptions of the activities.

Others took additional steps. For example, New York City published a summer activities booklet and launched an advertising campaign. Providence used flyers, recruitment fairs, advertising, parent-teacher organization meetings, and open houses to get its message out. In Chicago, the public schools disseminated a guide to available programs, and the libraries led an active teen marketing campaign.

In Providence, Washington, D.C., and Boston, the role of the site coordinator was key to working with principals and teachers to ensure that they understood and actively supported the programs and encouraged enrollment and regular attendance by students.

Ensure Affordability

A final potential stumbling block to enrollment might be cost or fees. In most of the cases here, the programs were available for free to the most in-need students, in part because of the strong efforts made by the agencies and intermediaries to obtain funding. For instance, in Providence, where there is very limited city funding for OST, PASA has continuously sought federal, state, and philanthropic funding to support programming. In 2008, PASA's board voted not to collect any fees for its OST programming, and PASA chose to focus more on securing 21st Century Learning Center grants (federal dollars managed by the Rhode Island Department of Education) to fund the AfterZones.

PASA has been successful in bringing in additional grants and support for Providence's coordinated OST effort beyond The Wallace Foundation and 21st Century funding. Providence's mayor has helped PASA secure federal Community Development Block Grant funding and introduced a line item in the city budget for after-school programming for the first time. PASA was particularly successful in raising private funding from multiple sources. However, braiding these funds together took a concerted effort, and interviewees in Providence noted that long-term sustainability remains a challenge.

Goal 2: Improve Quality

Leaders at the sites were aware that, prior to the initiative, some of the existing programming was not of high quality. Several sites concentrated significant effort on developing standards of provision, quality-assessment systems to monitor providers, and incentives and contractual mechanisms to ensure better provision, as well as on evaluating outcomes to drive improvement across the board (see Table 3.3). In addition, several sites invested in professional development for providers and the coordinators who were placed in the neighborhood schools to manage the programs. However, even after several years of effort, none claimed that the programs being offered were of universally high quality, nor could they demonstrate quantitative improvements in quality. Thus, while much was accomplished, work remains in this particular area.

Create Standards and Assessment Tools

Three of the sites (Washington, D.C., New York City, and Providence) developed and implemented a new set of standards and tools to assess providers. For instance, in Providence, PASA leadership

Table 3.3
Sites' Efforts to Improve Quality

Goal	Providence	New York City	Boston	Chicago	Washington, D.C.
Create standards and assessment tools	Created and publicly released	Used a modified version of NYSAN standards	New standards abandoned for existing Triumph Collaborative standards	Piloted newly developed standards in 2008–2009	Published guide to best practices in 2004
Monitor quality	Implemented in PASA and state providers	Implemented using NYSAN tool	New assessment abandoned for original PSS; now using existing Triumph Collaborative tool	Launched pilot in 2008 in Park District sites	Implemented for Trust-funded providers
Vet new providers	Through contract process	Through contract process		Through contract process	Through contract process 2009 in DCPS
Provide professional development	PASA provides professional development throughout state that is linked to the assessment tool	Given to all providers free of charge through intermediary contracted by city Intensive professional development provided to struggling providers	DELTAS offers coaching and professional development	Offered to quality pilot sites only	Provided to coordinators Trained nonprofit leaders
Provide performance incentives		Provider payment tied to attendance targets			
Evaluate progress	External evaluation ongoing	External evaluation ongoing	Ended external evaluation after first year		Informal only

felt that it was vital to develop quality measures through a community effort andengaged various groups to accomplish this goal. Starting in November 2004, a workgroup was assembled to consider quality. A group of approximately 25 participants considered already established standards from other cities and adapted them to meet Providence's needs. Interviewees told us that this workgroup created buy-in from providers and created an identity for Providence's after-school programming at a critical time prior to the formal launch of the AfterZones. The established standards are now used across the state of Rhode Island.

After standards were chosen, it became necessary to develop indicators and assessment tools. A smaller team met in late 2005 and early 2006 to develop these indicators and to consider an assessment tool. Participants included representatives from advocacy groups, staff from professional development nonprofits, and city officials, as well as representatives from some provider organizations. The discussion of indicators occurred in concert with the selection of an assessment tool. According to respondents, there was tension between advocates of a totally homegrown tool, reflective of the community planning effort to create quality standards and indicators, and advocates of a well-known tool that had more widespread recognition and credibility. Eventually, a hybrid tool, the Rhode Island Program Quality Assessment (RIPQA), was developed. The tool uses the HighScope Youth Program Quality Assessment's Form A (a valid instrument designed to evaluate the quality of youth programs at the point of service), and the PASA-developed Form B, which assesses organizational capacity.

Boston also worked to develop standards and an assessment tool, but after merging the PSS schools into the Triumph Collaborative, it ended up relying primarily on existing standards and assessments already used by the DELTAS office.

Chicago began implementing a program improvement pilot initiative in September 2009 in 43 OST program sites: two Chicago Public School sites, four After School Matters sites, four library sites, eight Park District sites, and 25 Family and Support Services sites. The pilot consisted of peer coaching, a self-administered program assessment, and an external assessment. Based on these assessments, program staff and their coach developed and implemented a program improvement plan. The program assessment tool used was a version of HighScope's Youth Program Quality Assessment that was customized for Chicago. The Chicago Area Project, a private nonprofit, focused on preventing delinquency and servicing disadvantaged urban youth, provided technical assistance and training to pilot sites, and oversaw the external evaluation process.

Monitor Quality and Vet Providers

Cities developed different mechanisms for monitoring quality. In Providence, PASA and outside evaluators from OST providers across the city and state used the assessment tool to conduct observations of the programs and to provide constructive feedback. Respondents there said that this process benefited the programs and raised the observers' awareness. The entire process was viewed as assistance and was not used punitively to reduce funding or eliminate the provider from the effort. In fact, interviewees described the process as a professional development tool for the community of providers.

In New York City, DYCD program managers used a modified version of the New York State Afterschool Network (NYSAN) Program Quality Self-Assessment tool to measure program quality during two site visits per year as a way to monitor the progress of OST programs and to ensure that they received the support they needed. When a program was struggling, program managers referred it to PASE, the technical assistance provider, for additional assistance and follow up.

The Trust began conducting regular quality assessments through its Project My Time site directors and staff in January 2008, and quality scores became a key criterion for future funding in September 2008. Meanwhile, DCPS put in place a formal vetting process for the providers with which it would contract, including a review of their basic health and safety certifications and curriculum.

Provide Professional Development and Performance Incentives

In Providence, professional development changed over the course of the implementation grant. Initially, professional development was not aligned with the developed program standards. Therefore, leaders thought it was not as effective as the more current offerings, although it did build some goodwill with providers. There were monthly workshops on such topics as parent engagement and staff retention, along with a 32-hour youth development certificate program known as the BEST (Building Exemplary Systems for Training Youth Works) youth worker program. But more recent PASA professional development for after-school providers now aligns with the various modules of the assessment tool (RIPQA). Programs not participating in RIPQA can still benefit from the training, which emphasizes practices to improve program quality that can apply to all programs (e.g., providing a safe and supportive environment, ensuring positive interactions with youth, promoting youth engagement).

In New York City, DYCD made a substantial financial investment in improving the quality of staff in the OST programs it funds. As the result of an RFP process, DYCD awarded PASE a three-year contract and provided $500,000 annually for a variety of training, technical assistance, and capacity-building opportunities for programs. These services were provided free of charge to organizations receiving DYCD OST funding. PASE offered a variety of professional development workshops and conferences throughout the year. In 2008, it also offered on-site training in Staten Island and Far Rockaway—two locations where participation by providers in centrally offered training had been low.

In New York City, interviewees noted that some programs were heavy users, or "frequent flyers," while other programs took advantage of professional development opportunities to a lesser extent. Many of these offerings helped fulfill programs' licensing requirements. PASE also solicited ideas for training from DYCD, OST program staff, and their consultants. In addition, PASE provided training and support for the use of MI systems.

For OST programs that failed to meet quality standards, PASE brokered targeted on-site technical assistance. After receiving a referral from a DYCD program manager, PASE would follow up with the program, conduct a needs assessment, and contract with one of its consultants to provide the needed technical assistance on site.

A new initiative in 2009 was to provide technical assistance in infrastructure and management to provider organizations operating a large number of programs (i.e., organizations that ran ten or more OST programs) to improve their internal operations and thus provide stronger services to students.

In addition to giving direct providers professional development, as described earlier, the Trust offered training to leaders of OST non-profits to get them to think about how to provide quality programs on a larger scale. This required a change in how the leaders of those organizations thought about and managed their operations.

In Boston, DELTAS employed coaches to assist the school site coordinator in a variety of capacities (e.g., parent engagement, leadership and supervision, curriculum, supporting English language learners). Each coach was in charge of between five and ten schools. One respondent described the coach as "extremely good at helping to professionalize what we do here. . . . He comes to partner meetings, [and] I meet [someone] at a networking event, and my coach says, 'Let me draft the MOU or work plan so there is a paper trail'—or other things that a lot of times schools or community organizations tend to gloss over." Universally, interviewees found the coaching extremely helpful.

Evaluate Progress

Finally, New York City and Providence hired outside evaluators to assess their efforts. Boston had also planned an outside evaluation but felt that it was too early for the evaluation, particularly considering the high turnover among key staff; thus, it ended its evaluation after the first year.

In Providence, the Center for Resource Management took an initial look at AfterZone outcomes in 2007 and reported on AfterZone participant demographics as well as linkages between school outcomes and AfterZone participation. Most significantly, the report showed that students who participated in PASA programs tended to have slightly higher rates of school attendance than nonparticipants. The report also indicated that PASA was not, in the words of one source, "skimming the cream," or attracting an atypical group of students as compared to the total Providence middle school population. At the time of our last site visit to Providence in spring 2009, Public/Private Ventures was in the midst of a three-year longitudinal study funded by The

Wallace Foundation that included surveys of AfterZone participants and nonparticipants.

In New York City, DYCD contracted with Policy Studies Associates to conduct a three-year evaluation of the OST initiative. DYCD appeared to be an active user of information that emerged from the evaluation. For instance, after the evaluation found that parents particularly liked and needed summer programs, DYCD made summer programming a requirement in the next round of RFPs. Interviewees throughout the system—from all levels of DYCD and leaders in the field—mentioned and referred to the Policy Studies Associates study. In 2009, DYCD remained committed to continuing the evaluation even in the face of potential budget cuts. As one DYCD official noted, "It has been important to maintain the core mission and the component parts, and that is quality direct services and also evaluation. Very often you say, 'Let's throw out the evaluation, the capacity building.' For us, that is not fluff; that is core."

Goal 3: Develop Information Systems for Decisionmaking

A major thrust of the initiative was to encourage the development of an MI system to track children and enrollment patterns. From the point of view of The Wallace Foundation, this was essential to understanding whether the programs were attracting children and whether the children's participation was frequent enough to affect their development. The cities made varying progress in the development of MI systems for student tracking purposes, but, as the systems were developed, the cities found important additional uses for the information. Data-based planning and communication strategies adopted to improve access and quality had multiplier effects and often generated greater coordination and communication. Additional details on this subject can be found in McCombs, Orr, et al., 2010.

All five cities devoted considerable energy to developing MI systems to track enrollment, participation, and student demographics. For instance, Chicago dedicated the majority of its effort in the early years to developing and implementing an MI system for the Park District, Chicago Public Schools, Family and Support Services, and After School Matters. Each organization had a customized system, but data from each could be easily merged to provide a comprehensive view of OST enrollment and attendance in Chicago.

During this period, four of the cities adopted and used an MI system that tracked student enrollment, attendance, and demographics. The exception was Boston, where an MI system that could be linked to the public schools data system was in development. The use of MI systems to track student enrollment, attendance, and demographics represented a major step forward for these four cities. For the first time, they knew across a large number of programs how many students were enrolled and attending on a regular basis as well as the characteristics of the students.

This simple step was particularly important for Providence, where surveys during the early planning period had shown that parents were reluctant to send their children to after-school programs unless the provider could ensure the child's safety, including knowing where the child was at all times. PASA used the system to allow it to track the children into and home from the programs on a daily basis, including on the buses. In this way, PASA could immediately determine the location of a child upon parent request.

These same four cities also used these systems to collect information about providers, including the type of programming offered, and used these data to determine which programs were attracting the most students and where they were located. This was most advanced in Providence and New York City. Again, the centralized data system was a first for these cities.

Several sites then sought to go further with data collection. For example, Washington, D.C., hoped to merge information about students' academic backgrounds with after-school attendance data to determine whether the children who attended had associated improvements in academic outcomes. Additionally, some hoped to merge the attendance data with information about each student's involvement in the juvenile justice system or family services, believing that this information would allow providers to craft supports to meet the child's particular needs.

However, practical and legal barriers prevented this from occurring, including the agencies' need to protect student records as required under state and federal human subject protections. Other practical barriers had to be overcome to develop the systems to this point. Funding and expertise needed for data collection and analysis was in short supply across the sites. Interviewees reported institutional inertia and turf issues that led to each agency favoring its own system and an unwillingness to share data with other agencies.

Compared to site reports on what existed prior to the initiative efforts, by the spring of 2009, sites were developing and using information for a range of purposes. All the sites, except Boston, were using an MI system to track daily attendance in OST programs and to understand some basic characteristics of who enrolled by program type and geographic location in the city.

Three cities took a further step to understand why children were attending different programs. Providence conducted surveys of the children as they proceeded through the programs. It used a combination of the survey and attendance data to identify problematic programs and to work with them to improve, as well as to develop new programs to meet the interests of the children. PASA provided its student survey information to its evaluator for use in assessing the impact of the programs on student motivation, aspiration, and engagement in school. New York City and Washington, D.C., used program attendance as a proxy for quality, assuming that children would vote with their feet and that poor-quality programs would be visible by poor attendance. Analysts reviewed attendance records to determine which programs seemed to have the biggest draw and ensured that these program types were offered. This approach also focused attention on programs with poor attendance, helping to understand why this was happening. In New York City, program providers were held accountable for achieving specific attendance goals and were paid accordingly. Washington, D.C., was considering such action.

Interviewees in New York City and Chicago noted that the use of an MI system shifted the nature of contracting, enabling agency staff to monitor programs and provide assistance to them on an ongoing basis. Without an MI system, contract officers received attendance reports on a quarterly or annual basis, and often on paper. Thus, it was difficult to identify struggling programs and impossible to provide assistance to help programs improve in a timely way. However, an MI system allowed agency officials to flag potential program problems early and intervene with assistance. OST providers also recognized this shift.

Finally, the ability to plan and advocate was seen by many as an important unforeseen outcome of the MI system development effort. In Providence, New York City, and Washington, D.C., information collected from the attendance systems and the surveys was used to effectively advocate for stable or increased funding for after-school programs. Armed with data and evidence that funds were being spent more efficiently but demand remained (i.e., that poor providers were being weeded out, programs were being located in the highest-need areas, and demand remained), agency heads and intermediaries began to argue for increased funding and city support. When city agencies that competed for funding could not show similar progress in moving toward accountability or proof of needed services, the after-school agencies won greater funding, especially in New York City and Providence. Seeing the data, the mayors could argue that they were fulfilling their campaign promises and began to demand these data.

In summary, the development and use of student tracking systems, student surveys, and provider information proved to be key parts of building a more coordinated effort to meet the initiative's goals. Information was used to support improved access by offering programs of interest to students and ensuring that they were located where students could access them. In Providence, it was also used to ensure that students were safe and supervised. The information was also used to improve quality by identifying programs with little student support and by providing professional development or needed training and holding providers responsible for improved attendance, as in New York City. In at least a few instances, such systems were responsible for providing needed data that could be used to argue for increased funding, and work on the development of the system itself encouraged collaboration and coordination that had not occurred before. In short, the development and use of systemwide information that had been almost nonexistent prior to this effort added significantly to the initiative.

Goal 4: Plan for Financial Sustainability

Sustainability here refers to both sustaining the collaborative effort and sustaining the programmatic funding levels needed to meet the initiative plans for expansion, although we heavily emphasize the latter. We reviewed sites' plans for sustainment of both the collaborative effort and the funding. The activities they described fell into four areas (see Table 3.4). In planning and developing more stable funding or funding for growth, the plans talked of finding new funding sources and activities designed to maintain general public support. In ensuring that coordination was maintained, they pointed to clarifying roles across the organizations and activities or embedding coordination into the system's structures, such as MOUs or contractual relationships. The sites were struggling with issues of financial sustainment when the study ended. Several had sought new funding sources, such as local and national foundations or federal funds for 21st Century Community Learning Centers. However, all faced uncertain funding prospects in spring 2009.

The five cities used a combination of resources to support current programming but relied primarily on government contracts and foundation grants. PASA in Providence had moved to ensure stronger funding by helping several CBOs gain federal 21st Century Learning Center status through grant writing and providing data to support the proposal. New York City had increased funding based on the strong support of the mayor and the clear evidence of effectiveness. And discussions among ICSIC members in Washington pushed DCPS after-school program managers to reallocate some internal resources to increase funding.

At the time of our spring 2009 visit, the sites reported struggling with sustainment of program funding. Several of the cities were forecasting reduced budgets, and the various leads were pursuing the means to at least hold steady if not grow in the coming months.

Table 3.4
Sites' Efforts to Improve Sustainability

Goal	Providence	New York City	Boston	Chicago	Washington, D.C.
Obtain new funding sources	National foundations 21st Century funding Fees from provision of services statewide	Successfully used new data to argue for increased city funding	Unsuccessfully sought city and local foundation funding		DCPS began to reallocate resources to support programming
Generate public support	Generate data and publicize success	Generate data and publicize success	Planning 2010 communication campaign and presentation of program gaps	Planning outreach strategy to garner greater state support for OST funding	Generate data and publicize success
Provide clear organizational roles	Consistent lead and roles	Consistent lead and roles documented in MOUs	Shifting lead agencies	Consistent lead and roles	Shifting lead agency and roles
Maintain partner interest	PASA convenes city leads under mayor to address high school OST City agencies remain on PASA board and now have own steering committee to coordinate city resources	Contractual arrangements and professional development ensure buy-in MOUs ensure link with city's Department of Education and DYCD	Partner involvement evolving; new focus on CLI	MI system builds interest Partners actively engaged in creating new vision Steering committee remains active	Leads shift but partners remain interested because ICSIC breeds partner interest in issues of concern to mayor

Three of the five sites thought in similar terms. Downturns in city budgets had occurred before, and agency leaders we interviewed thought that the best way to address them was to argue for the effectiveness of the programs in meeting important city goals, such as reduced crime and increased graduation. Therefore, in rough times, they thought that the data from the MI system and from any evaluation that showed increased effectiveness could be used to argue for the programs' value. Washington, D.C., New York City, and Providence, in particular, sought to generate information on both the effectiveness of the programs and the growing efficiency of their operations and to publicize these results. In addition, they sought to engage community leaders and parents in support of the programs to act as advocates with city hall. Mayors who were strongly supportive of the programs to begin with, armed with data showing their effectiveness, would see them through—or so these leaders hoped.

Chicago's sustainability efforts focused on securing dedicated funding for after-school programs at the state level. Given the state's budget crisis, this effort seems unlikely to bear fruit in the short term, although sources hastened to point out that it was still necessary so that after-school funding would someday be "first in line" when economic conditions and budgetary conditions improved. Boston's efforts to establish a sustainability plan were delayed due to reorganization of the initiative.

In terms of maintaining collaboration across organizations in pursuit of the initiative's goals, most interviewees in New York City and Chicago assumed their programs would survive as long as strong outcomes persisted because they had become embedded in the routine of government agencies. For example, New York City had established an MOU with its Department of Education, which provided school facilities free of charge to OST programs. The MOU helped ensure that this collaboration would continue into the future. In addition, New York City had embedded coordination in the contractual arrangements it made with providers, ensuring that providers were evaluated and received professional development to improve. Chicago was considering such options, and with its new MI systems and piloting of its quality standards was maintaining the interest of the various organizations.

Providence's efforts, however, were led by an intermediary organization. PASA chose to use its success to increase its presence and cement further relations at the state level and to begin offering its professional development and quality-assurance services at other sites across the state by pooling resources. In addition, Providence was moving toward expanding programming into the high school arena, with strong support from the mayor. A new coordinating group had been established in his office that brought together the major city agencies that might have the resources to support after-school programs, such as facilities or buses, in an effort to identify efficiencies that could generate additional revenues for provision. The coordinating role of the intermediary, with support from the mayor and other agency heads, appeared to sustain and support growth.

Boston and Washington, D.C., were also led by intermediaries, but these organizations had not been successful in leading the efforts for reasons discussed previously. In these two cities, the nature of further collaboration was unclear, as was the role that intermediaries would play. At the time of our visits in spring 2009, while work was under way in the public schools to improve coordinated services, the level of interorganizational coordination between city and noncity agencies was undergoing change. For example, in Boston, respondents were starting to focus on the CLI as the means to promote collaboration among schools, the libraries, and the parks and recreational centers. Respondents in both cities expressed uncertainty about how these types of coordinated efforts would be sustained.

In summary, we found all the sites struggling with issues of funding, several struggling with continued collaboration, and all preparing for a difficult year or two as budgets tightened.

Summary

In this chapter, we described what the sites did to address the initiative's expectations regarding access, quality, use of information for decisionmaking, and sustained funding. We reviewed the cities' progress made by comparing the statements from early proposals and interviewees aware of early efforts to later similar sources in spring 2009.

Access. Sites addressed issues of convenience and lack of access by locating additional programs in neighborhood schools, attempting to provide transportation, developing online program locaters, and marketing programs to target populations. The number of children served expanded in most of the cities. Further, the initiatives addressed transportation and convenience issues of parents, thereby increasing access in Washington, D.C., New York City, and Providence.

Quality. Several sites concentrated significant effort on developing standards of provision, quality-assessment systems for providers, and incentives and contractual mechanisms to ensure better provision. In addition, several sites invested in professional development for the providers and for coordinators placed in the neighborhood schools to manage the programs.

Information for Decisionmaking. A few cities invested in evaluations of their efforts, some of which included student outcomes, and all the cities devoted considerable energy to developing MI systems to track enrollment, participation, and demographics. Several developed systems to collect information about providers and to determine which programs were attracting students. While gathering program data of this type may seem commonplace, this was the first time these cities had such systems and could begin to plan more effectively to increase and improve provision. Data-based planning and communication strategies adopted to improve access and quality had multiplier effects and often generated greater coordination and communication.

Sustainability. The sites were struggling with issues of financial sustainment when the study ended. Several had sought new funding sources, such as local and national foundations or federal funds for 21st Century Community Learning Centers. Three of the sites used data to develop "success stories" to help maintain public support for programming. Sites attempted to maintain partnerships by delineating clear roles among organizations and embedding the coordination in an MOU, shared MI systems, contractual arrangement, and elsewhere.

However, all faced uncertain funding prospects in spring 2009 that might threaten further collaboration.

CHAPTER FOUR

Enabling Coordinated System-Building Efforts

The Wallace Foundation's premise was that collaborative approaches across organizations within a city would help enable the creation of a more effective and coordinated OST program. Here, we discuss whether and how the sites used collaborative approaches to enable the initiative to move forward (answering research question 3). Similar to the approach in the previous chapter, we relied on the sites to tell us how they approached collaboration across organizations and agencies and what enabled it. We then placed that information into categories developed from the literature.

The sites used different means to achieve more coordination. Respondents thought that these collaborative mechanisms enabled progress, and, in several sites, the mechanisms became embedded in the new structures and policy supports of the evolving system. New and better-aligned structures, new MOUs, and data and analytic capabilities all became the part of the systems put in place to support the goals.

The interviewees were adamant about several factors that acted as enablers of coordinated system building, some of which were identified in the literature. These factors included whether the site created a common vision during the early planning phase; effectively collected and used data and information; received strong, supportive, stable leadership, especially in the mayor's office; and gained the active support of the schools. Wallace Foundation funding as an investment and the role of funding generally also enabled coordinated system building. We found that system-building activities bore fruit when all these factors were present. When the shared vision and the active support of the mayor were missing, we found that reported activities were stalled and courses of actions changed.

This chapter first discusses the use of general collaborative mechanisms to develop greater coordination and then highlights specific enablers and inhibitors raised during interviews at the sites.

How Cities Used Cross-Organizational Collaboration to Support Greater Coordination

The literature described a set of activities that social service agencies have used in collaborative efforts to improve services. We adopted them to the OST setting and list them in the first column of Table 4.1. We then used the descriptions provided by the sites to fill in the cells with the specific activities undertaken in each site. Some of these points have already been discussed in prior chapters. For example, Chapter Two showed how early planning and coordination were crucial to identifying targets, consolidating resources and powers, and developing later plans. It also described how sites consolidated or changed structures to improve coordination. These are included in Table 4.1 as activities or mechanisms that enabled greater coordination.

Table 4.1 shows that Providence and New York City undertook many collaborative activities to promote coordinated system building. As discussed later, the early planning efforts described in Chapter Two brought agencies and stakeholder groups, such as providers and parents, into discussions about how the system could be improved and what the initiative would attempt. Interviewees noted that this built tremendous buy-in and goodwill for the initiative. Washington, D.C., undertook a similar effort in the early years when the Trust led the effort. However, with mayoral takeover, the lead role shifted to DCPS, and the nature of collaboration shifted from larger public engagement to intra-agency collaboration.

These three sites successfully put in place consolidation efforts or created new organizations to address OST issues, developed mechanisms to ensure regular meetings of interested parties, made significant

Table 4.1
Collaborative Mechanisms Used to Support Coordinated Systems

Activity	Providence	New York City	Boston	Chicago	Washington, D.C.
Performed early cross-organizational analysis to identify needed citywide provision	Planning-year efforts involved all major stakeholders and identified middle school youth as most underserved	Planning-year efforts involved major stakeholders and identified locations in the city that lacked programs; supported by role of special adviser	Minimal early efforts identified low-performing schools but did not enjoin all stakeholders	Early efforts focused on city agencies that provided OST, with no broader community or provider input	Trust planning efforts involved all stakeholders and identified middle school provision as needing improvement
Worked collaboratively across stakeholders and agencies to build shared goals	Early forums aired issues and helped build stakeholder consensus on middle school students; now using same process to develop high school initiative	Mayor kicked off series of forums to discuss issues and build consensus among agencies and organizations around goals for OST	Not part of early efforts, which were confined to a few organizational leaders. Later, mayor's subcabinet meetings begin to build collaboration. CLI initiative beginning to involve three agencies to work on common goals	Worked across agencies to build MI systems using committee structure; now addressing quality-improvement processes through a pilot	The Trust initially led effort to engage external shareholders; mayoral takeover and formation of ICSIC changed focus to coordination across city agencies
Consolidated functions or structures and clarified roles	New intermediary (PASA) created to lead	Consolidated city funded after-school programs for in-need youth in DYCD during planning period	Very little clarity of roles as the initiative restructured		

Table 4.1—Continued

Activity	Providence	New York City	Boston	Chicago	Washington, D.C.
Established regular, routine means to coordinate among organizations	Established coordination through PASA board, which meets regularly and includes stakeholder groups Later added city agency coordinating meetings	Established routine meetings of agencies involved led by the special adviser	Mayor established subcabinet meetings of youth-serving organizations	Established several cross-city agency committees that meet regularly	Mayor established and oversees regular ICSIC meetings
Developed information and means to share it to improve efforts	Developed, implemented, and shared, with new uses being found	Developed, implemented, and shared, with new uses being found	Under development	Data collected and structure developed; first run of system was about to be shared in spring 2009	Developed and placed in DCPS and shared with ICSIC agencies
Developed common incentives and supporting policies to ensure provider engagement in improvement	Established standards and implemented support policies to ensure quality improvement	Established standards, incentives, and supports for provider improvement	Offered professional development and coaching to Triumph Collaborative schools	Piloting quality-improvement standards and related training	Established standards and was beginning to use incentives in DCPS's and the Trust's efforts to improve provider quality
Sought and developed superintendent and principal buy-in/cooperation	Ensured through mayoral selection of new superintendent, who agreed with initiative Coordinators build principal buy-in	Ensured through the development and promulgation of MOUs with city's Department of Education	Worked to ensure principal buy-in for 10 PSS sites	OST programs already operating in schools, so not a major thrust of work	Coordinators hired by DCPS to build school buy-in

progress in developing shared data that could be used in such meetings to discuss how to improve, and created standards, incentives, and training as a means of coordinating with providers. In addition, each recognized the need to continually engage the superintendent and school staff. Providence and Washington, D.C., developed the position of a site coordinator to interact at the site level with school staff and the provider in engaging students in the programs, ensuring that the programs ran smoothly. New York City established MOUs at the agency level to ensure availability of space for after-school programming in schools.

Due to the fact that one agency did not control the majority of OST programming in the city, all of Chicago's efforts required multi-agency coordination and cooperation. Planners specifically selected the development of MI systems as the focus of early efforts because the systems were viewed as a positive first collaborative project for the agencies and because they provided a very tangible reward to partners for their cooperation and commitment. Building from that success, Chicago moved to adopt a quality pilot that involved all of the agencies. However, as of spring 2009, the collaborative efforts had not taken on any potentially contentious issues, such as the allocation of OST resources throughout the city or potential consolidation of programs.

In the initial two years of the grant, Boston's collaborative efforts focused almost exclusively at the school level on the PSS sites—establishing on-site coordinators and other efforts to link after-school programs to the school day. However, it undertook few activities that effectively coordinated actors and organizations outside of the schools. In spring 2009, we saw evidence of increased collaboration that was led by the mayor's office—the CLI and the mayor's subcabinet.

The Importance of Establishing a Common Vision

As part of the planning process, most cities worked to develop a commonly held vision of what they wanted to accomplish across stakeholders, including city agencies, the provider community, the schools and central office, and parents. In some cities, this process required the active involvement of key stakeholders, and, in one, there was less stakeholder engagement with important negative consequences.

As an example of the former, during the planning phase, New York City formed working groups organized around key topics, such as professional development, quality, and cost. Each of the six working groups consisted of advocates, providers, academics, and funders. Each working group submitted reports to the city with its recommendations. Hundreds of people participated in this process. We were told that the goal was to make the planning process inclusive so that all stakeholders would have a voice. Based on the working groups' efforts and internal coordination, DYCD issued a concept paper on OST and solicited comments from the field. While not all stakeholders supported every aspect of New York City's OST vision, it was clearly communicated, and key stakeholders reported to us that their buy-in was high at the end of the process.

Similarly, Providence undertook an extensive community-based engagement effort during the planning process in which the mayor convened more than 100 after-school leaders, city officials, students, and parents. While some stakeholders were disappointed when the grant focused on middle schools, support for what was done was relatively high, and the goals were well understood. The mayor had established enough credibility in the community that his promise to move to high school provision next was viewed as credible, leading to continued support across the area's provider community.

Early efforts in Washington, D.C., prior to the new administration's mayoral takeover of the schools, resembled those in Providence, with a significant focus on consensus building. After the new administration came into office, broader sets of stakeholders were less visible in the coordination efforts that focused primarily on government agencies through ICSIC. Similarly, Chicago's efforts focused on governmental interagency coordination, initially around the MI system development.

In contrast, in the initial years of the grant, Boston Beyond did not engage community stakeholders in the development of its PSS model or develop a common vision of system building under PSS. Significant staff turnover during this period likely contributed to this lack of outreach. Because a systemic vision of PSS was not communicated, respondents outside the PSS initiative said that they did not understand how PSS could be a system-building effort; instead, a few respondents described it as a "boutique" program found in a small number of schools. Respondents outside the PSS initiative also described resentment in the community that the grant money was not funding OST programs outside the PSS sites. Comments such as these showed the general lack of understanding of the purpose of the grant, as initiative funds were not allowed to be used for OST programming.

The Impact of Data and Information

We discovered that cities' efforts to gather data through needs assessments, market research, MI systems, and evaluation created greater coordination (organizations worked to gather and review additional data) and more data-based decisionmaking. Chicago and Washington, D.C., might provide the clearest examples of this phenomenon.

In Chicago, the effort to build MI systems that could easily merge all agencies' data brought city agency staff together on a regular basis and, from this process, working relationships grew. Over time, interviewees indicated that they began to see a benefit in the coordinated efforts in terms of shared goals and potentially more effective resource allocation, although by the end of this investigation, that remained largely a vision and not yet a reality.

Similarly, ICSIC in Washington, D.C., along with the mayor's budget office, ensured that the agencies worked together to develop a vision of strong OST services for youth. It was the data from the MI systems that allowed them to actually consider in concrete terms how to move forward and encouraged specific discussions about improvement.

In Providence, the use of the MI system helped the OST system flourish in that its practical uses allowed parents to feel comfortable sending their children to AfterZones, which likely encouraged student enrollment and participation. Using enrollment and participation data, along with student surveys, allowed the planners to begin addressing quality and programming issues, something that would benefit the children. These benefits, along with a collegial approach to problem solving, kept the many stakeholders at the table and involved.

In several instances, data from the MI system and evaluations led to changes in program funding and better policies. The resulting availability of data and analyses then allowed several mayors to publicly proclaim some early successes, which, in turn, drove them to demand data analyses on a regular basis. This ensured that agencies would seek to maintain and use data analyses for decisionmaking.

Boston, on the other hand, had not generated much usable data as of spring 2009. It was still working to develop an MI system and had not continued with an evaluation. Thus, it is not surprising that we did not find evidence of data-based decisions or collaboration fueled by data and information.

The Crucial Role of the Mayor

As noted previously, leadership and, particularly, the support and actions of mayors and their representatives were key enablers of system building. In New York City, mayoral support was critical to successful change within the bureaucracy. The OST initiative shifted resources between several agencies and demanded better coordination and communication among them. Because it was clear that the mayor wanted this initiative to succeed, agencies were forced to communicate, share information, and cooperate with one another. He signaled his interest in the initiative by designating a point person with the authority to coordinate the agencies' efforts. We were told by those involved in the planning process that the mayor's special adviser "was instrumental in pulling together [the commissioners] around a unified goal." When the planning process was over and the special adviser had stepped down, City Hall appointed a replacement to serve as a liaison among the agencies to keep the pressure on for coordination. The mayor also signaled his support for the initiative at press events and in state-of-the-city speeches. Perhaps the clearest signal was that he placed OST as a baseline item in the city's five-year financial plan.

PASA in Providence benefited from continued support from the mayor, who became a nationally recognized advocate of quality OST offerings. Respondents also noted that the leadership of PASA itself was capable, energetic, and committed. The mayor's reform agenda and support for integrated OST provision—in combination with well-qualified PASA leadership—was a significant factor in PASA's success. The chief of police and superintendent, both of whom were strong advocates and contributors to the system, joined the mayor in supporting OST.

Many interviewees in Chicago remarked on the value of having the city's first family initiate the effort through statements by the mayor and the role of the mayor's wife as head of After School Matters. There was, however, no push in Chicago to restructure, as there was in New York City. The coordination took place among agencies and focused initially on developing the MI systems on a largely voluntary basis. It seems that, because the multiple agencies involved in OST provision were all relatively powerful, interagency coordination was built on goodwill rather than a dictate from the mayor. It is difficult to tell whether greater active support by the mayor could have moved efforts further.

While a number of key leadership positions changed hands in Washington during the initiative (the mayor, superintendent, and president of the Trust), it still weathered these transitions and maintained supportive and productive leadership for OST. These changes altered the environment and priorities for OST in Washington, D.C., and made it difficult to implement the plan envisioned in the Wallace grant. The commitment toward expanding OST opportunities for students, however, remained high due to the involvement and actions of the new leadership in the mayor's office. In fact, many significant improvements in the OST system resulted from the focus of ICSIC, led by the mayor, and included the expansion of OST opportunities to students in all DCPS schools, a demand for data to drive the system, and the establishment of a vetting process for OST providers in DCPS schools.

In Boston, mayoral role both enabled and hindered progress. The mayor had always been a strong advocate for OST programming, and he led the charge to create Boston Beyond. While he remained committed to OST in the city, we were told that in the first two years of the PSS initiative, his strategy and that of the then–executive director of Boston Beyond became unaligned. The result was a rift between the two, and some respondents said that people in the OST community perceived that the mayor lost confidence in the leadership of the intermediary. This lack of alignment and loss of connection made it difficult for Boston Beyond to lead system-building activities.

Since the business plan was revised and a new executive director of Boston Beyond was hired, the mayor's support of the intermediary and its leadership returned. Indeed, the collaborative mechanisms and work described in spring 2009—the CLI and the interagency subcabinet of youth agencies—were both developed from the mayor's office. In addition, the mayor made OST a top campaign issue in his reelection bid. However, it is not at all clear whether the approach taken by the other sites that encouraged early needs assessment, building of stakeholder buy-in, and the development of a unifying information system would be undertaken.

Buy-In of the Schools

Most respondents in the sites emphasized that the role of the superintendent, central office staff, and principals was crucial to the effort, primarily because so many of the after-school activities would take place in the schools. After-school planners needed to ensure that providers had access to the schools, that facilities would be open, and that responsibility for maintenance, heating, cooling, and insurance would rest with the schools. They also needed to ensure that teachers and principals would work with the providers and encourage students to attend the programs. Thus, while active support by the superintendent or his or her office was desirable, at a minimum, planners needed basic support.

This was found in most sites, although in varying forms. For example, the MOU between the New York City Department of Education and DYCD guaranteed OST programs free access to a specific number of schools during the school year and in the summer; the Department of Education would fund the extended-use fees (i.e., the cost of operating schools after hours and during the 20 school holidays when they would typically be closed), security, fingerprinting of staff, and snacks. However, the chancellor's office was not heavily involved in the conceptual work of the initiative. In Providence, after the initial superintendent left, the mayor ensured that the process for selecting a new superintendent would emphasize the need to support PASA and the operation of middle school programs. In Washington, D.C., after the mayoral takeover, the superintendent's office took on the lead in pushing for improved programming and access. It was this active championing that moved the effort forward in that city.

Thus, we conclude that there are many roles that superintendents and their offices can play, but, at a minimum, they had to support the idea of after-school programming in their buildings and ensure the cooperation of the schools.

The cooperation of and coordination with the schools was not guaranteed, even with active involvement of the superintendent. Thus, several cities, including Providence, Washington, D.C., and Boston, created the position of a school-level coordinator to ensure full school cooperation, active recruiting efforts for after-school programming, and coordination between school-day and after-school activities. From the point of view of the program planners, this role was essential in ensuring high-functioning programs. Administrators in all three cities pointed out the differences among schools in their buy-in and support contingent on the specific skills and talents of the coordinator and, therefore, tried to hire the best candidates for these roles and provided them with professional development.

While this type of position was not used across all sites, respondents tended to agree that cooperation from the schools, principals, and teachers was important to a strong after-school program and saw uncooperative staff as a barrier to overcome in pursuit of increasing access and quality.

The Need for Investment and Other Funding Issues

Funding was and remains a crucial enabler of improving OST systems, and a lack of it remains a constant constraint. Each of the sites was struggling at the end of our study to deal with city budget deficits and possible reductions in philanthropic support that would affect their funding streams. This situation reflects the struggle faced by such programs on a regular basis, which is what motivated The Wallace Foundation's goal of addressing financial sustainability. None of the sites "solved" the financial sustainability issue. However, our study does provide some specific insights about funding issues, especially the need for investment funding, how it could be used, and the issue of stovepiped funding sources, which bedeviled some sites.

The Wallace Foundation made major investments in these cities, and interviewees were clear that without its support, in terms of funding and the challenge of the initiative, they would not have made as much progress. Each of these sites, unlike others throughout the country, received significant funding for needed large investments in personnel time and infrastructure. Site respondents reported that this was a major enabler, but using the funding in an effective manner was crucial as well.

Because all the sites received the funding and used it for a variety of purposes, we cannot say how much was enough. In general, funds paid for the time of market researchers, the administration of surveys, the running of community forums, development of quality assessment instruments, and professional development. It paid for the time of the early planners, coordinators, and leaders. In addition, it was used to develop the MI systems that proved to be a crucial step forward in four of the sites.

There were some contrasts in the payoff on sites' investments. For example, Chicago used much of the funding to build its MI systems, and New York City dedicated at least some of the funding to the role of the special adviser. Both investments appeared to pay off from the point of view of respondents. This contrasted with several investments in evaluation, a child assessment tool, and a set of quality standards made by Boston Beyond in the early years of the Boston initiative, which went unused during later efforts led by DELTAS after the restructuring.

We described the result of The Wallace Foundation investment that helped cities develop some "system infrastructure," but at the conclusion of the research, the sites were struggling for regular operating funds in the midst of a recession and considering whether they would need to cut back on slots or personnel in the near future. Clearly, lack of funding is a major constraint on improving programming, but several sites also noted the continuing challenge of "braiding together" funding from different sources that had dedicated uses. For example, the sites received funding from a variety of sources, including U.S. Department of Education Title I funds, U.S. Department of Education 21st Century Community Learning Center grants, federal Temporary Assistance to Needy Families, state and city funds, and philanthropic donations. Each has specific rules and regulations about what the funds can be used for and under what conditions. A considerable amount of personnel time went into figuring out how to effectively braid the funding streams in supportive packages. In other words, funding itself required significant attention to coordination and considerable adeptness in determining which programs could receive which funds or which student could receive which funds to make the overall system work. Planners felt that this fragmentation of funding was a major constraint on providing a more coordinated system and that this would continue to be the case.

Summary

In summary, the sites used many different collaborative mechanisms to increase coordination across evolving systems. These coordination mechanisms acted as enablers of progress and, in some ways, became embedded in the new structures and policy supports of the evolving system of OST provision. New, better-aligned structures, new MOUs, data and analytic capabilities, and quality-improvement mechanisms all became the part of the system put in place to support the goals of better OST provision.

The cases provide numerous examples that other sites could follow to help build better system supports. While the investment funding provided by The Wallace Foundation was essential, alone, it was not enough to ensure coordination or progress toward the goals of the initiative: At least one site did not make significant progress despite the funding provided. Interviewees emphasized that a shared vision, early planning and the building of the MI systems, mayoral support, and buy-in from the schools were important enablers to move the sites toward the goals of the initiative. Lack of several of these posed significant challenges to coordination. Importantly, lack of funding or fragmented funding streams remained an important constraint to building more coordinated systems. While support from the mayor and superintendent and investments in coordination can, and did in several of these sites, pay off, the sites continued to face constant challenges to improvement.

The question then remains how to ensure that other cities have some of the enablers that these cities did. While we have documented clear steps to take—the actions of the mayors and the steps taken in the early days to ensure some consensus—we do not think that the process can be mechanistically replicated. The cases serve as examples of what can be done, but they are not blueprints. Further, we do not have insights into how other cities can obtain the investment funds needed. These cases do, however, hint at what other cities might be able to accomplish and the process they may want to undertake should investments be made.

CHAPTER FIVE

Lessons for Other Cities

The comparative case study approach yielded rich details and increased understanding of the pathways, processes, and hypotheses that can be tested in the future. This analysis provided useful comparative information about what cities can do to address shortfalls in access or quality of after-school provision and how some cities have built MI systems and strived for sustainable funding. Our analysis showed that the context of each city mattered in what it chose to focus on. It also confirmed much of the literature in terms of what would prove to be important for progress. It provided evidence on very specific actions that mayors could take to push their efforts forward. The companion monograph on the building of MI systems, *Hours of Opportunity*, Volume 2: *The Power of Data to Improve After-School Programs Citywide* (McCombs, Orr, et al., 2010), makes clear how strong leadership manifests.

The descriptions herein, and those in McCombs, Orr, et al. (2010) and McCombs, Bodilly, et al. (2010), provide concrete examples for others to consider based on the approaches of The Wallace Foundation grantees, their reasons for taking these approaches, and the proximate result—the immediate effect on OST provision, structure, access, quality-assurance processes, information for planning, and sustainability. We now summarize some themes from the analysis that other cities might consider.

Coordinated system-building efforts can work to improve access and quality. The analysis showed that these cities' coordinated attempts at system improvement were effective in meeting several goals. Through their efforts, four cities increased the number of students served by OST programs. For example, in Providence, OST program enrollment increased from 500 to 1,700 middle schoolers under this initiative, and New York City increased the number of slots from 45,000 to 80,000. Programs were located in all DCPS schools in Washington, D.C., and, in Boston, five schools began to offer after-school programs where none had existed before. In each case, these efforts targeted high-need student populations. Essential to this progress were early needs assessments, development of program locators for use by parents and students, and student tracking information to determine program demand and student locations.

While we cannot at this point determine whether quality improved, each of the cities used the investment funds to begin or put in place quality-assessment systems, including developing and promulgating standards, vetting and assessing providers against the standards, offering professional development to improve staff expertise and programming, and using contractual clauses to ensure that participation goals were met. Crucial to these efforts was the development and use of MI systems to track student demand for programs and the use of student and parent surveys to obtain opinions about quality.

While the sites made progress in obtaining more sustained funding (for example, by winning 21st Century Community Learning Center awards), unfortunately, this study took place at a time of great national financial upheaval. The sites struggled with ways to ensure steady funding, but uncertainty remained. Nevertheless, the respondents thought that their efforts to improve system building before the economic downturn put them in better positions to argue for sustained funding by allowing them to show progress toward outcomes, and more efficient use of resources was already under way.

This initiative provided a proof of principle—that organizations across cities could work together toward increasing access, quality, data-based decisionmaking, and sustainability. The final impact, however, remains unknown until the evaluations undertaken by the sites are published.

Each city has a unique context that should drive what is attempted. City context influenced the focus, scope, and lead for the system-building work. Early planning efforts revealed different needs and challenges in the cities and influenced some cities to focus on a particular target population, such as middle school students.

Cities varied in organization of the effort, with some being led by intermediaries and others a government agency. In cities in which an agency provided significant funding for OST, a city agency was designated as lead. In cities with a low level of city funding for OST, an intermediary took on the lead role. These few examples do not lead us to view one approach as preferable to another. Instead, it seems that, again, context matters. The lesson for other cities is that the decision about who will lead the effort and the structure of coordination needs to take into account the assets at hand, the locus of control, and the skills and talents of leaders. It seems unlikely that the Providence intermediary-led model would have worked in New York City with its strongly independent, multiple, and uncoordinated city agencies. But neither would the New York City agency-led model work in Providence, which lacked city agencies involved in after-school programming.

In summary, each city's initiative differed due to its unique circumstances. Other cities will need to consider their own circumstances before deciding what might best propel their efforts forward.

Investments in early planning and management information system development paid off. These sites were given a unique opportunity because The Wallace Foundation investment allowed them to carefully consider what needed to be done across the city for improvement to take place. They deliberated the specific assets in place, the organizations involved, the challenges faced, and the funding available. Investments in the early planning phase paid high dividends in clearly identifying targets for improvement and beginning to develop a means of sharing information to promote better decisionmaking across the city.

Similarly, investments in MI systems and evaluations helped the actors understand whether progress was made and allowed them to argue more effectively for additional funding. Furthermore, all this work brought together different actors, often for the first time, to discuss how to build a better OST system. While building information systems was a major goal of the effort, these systems also became a major enabler of further progress on access and quality as well as the glue that led to cooperation and coordination in a couple of cities.

Cities should definitely consider early data gathering to help inform their efforts. These sites offer examples of the types of information collected and how it could be used to propel efforts forward. The major caveat is that it must be shared across organizations and stakeholders to improve system-building efforts.

Cities can consider an array of approaches to improving access and quality. The sites we studied found an array of ways to meet their goals to increase access and improve quality. Some part of successfully improving access had to do with identifying underserved areas and students and finding the mechanisms to provide convenient access, such as placement of programs in neighborhood hubs, providing transportation to and from the programs, program locators, and free programs.

Cities attempted to improve quality through the adoption of standards, the use of the standards to assess program quality, provision of professional development, and evaluating their own efforts. A major difference among the grantees was whether the lead chose to use contractual means to hold the providers accountable for improving quality (as in New York City, with DCPS in Washington, D.C., possibly following suit) or whether the lead used more collegial means, such as significant professional development or joint reflection on quality, as in Providence, Chicago, and Washington, D.C., under the Trust. Again, this is an important choice and depends on city context. Importantly, Providence chose this path, as did the Trust, because its early planning efforts showed a scarcity of providers. Planners in these organizations thought that developing better existing resources was a more viable pathway to quality and access than driving poor providers out of the system.

Again, the major lesson is that context is important and should be considered carefully when developing approaches to increasing access and improving quality.

Cities can consider an array of mechanisms for increased coordination. The sites used an array of mechanisms to improve coordination. Efforts included early planning that brought multiple organizations together, engaging stakeholders to build shared goals, restructuring and consolidating roles, establishing coordinating committees or steering committees, and other regular means to share information and decisions. One used the appointment of mayoral envoys to ensure interagency cooperation or the development of interagency MOUs. It was in the instance of Boston, which did not undertake these types of activities to the same extent in early years of the grant and which changed lead organizations, that coordination occurred in fits and starts. Several of these steps proved to be most important from the interviewees' point of view, and we describe them as enablers in the next section.

Several enablers were important. Interviewees agreed on several important enablers of collaborative efforts. They were the building of a common vision across stakeholders in the early planning period, effectively collecting and using data and information, supportive mayoral actions, the buy-in of the schools, and investment funding.

Wallace Foundation staff clearly recognized these potential enablers as they developed the initiative. The Foundation provided early planning grants to encourage sites to conduct early needs assessments and establish a shared vision for the work that informed their business plans. It required the adoption of MI systems to create an ongoing source of data for the cities. Indeed, cities with strong needs assessments, a strong vision shared by stakeholders across the system, and MI systems made significant progress toward their goals.

In addition, The Foundation selected cities based, in part, on evidence of mayoral support. Mayoral support was key to the progress made in these cities, but it took on forms far beyond simple encouragement and bully pulpit statements. Getting a mayor actively involved will be challenging in many cities. Educating the mayor early in the process about how he or she can affect the outcomes by reorganizing agency responsibilities or realigning funding sources and by demanding data on progress might be an additional strong investment with a high payoff later.

Ensuring the support of the schools appeared to be a complex process and one that was ongoing, taking significant time and resources. Not only was it necessary to ensure the cooperation of the central office to allow access to schools free of charge, it was necessary to ensure that principals and staff actively supported the programs and encouraged children to attend. This process took concerted effort and was aided in several cities by a school site coordinator whose job, among other tasks, was to actively engage the school staff. The capabilities of these coordinators were crucial in enabling effective program offerings and operations. Thus, a solution was found, but it was dependent on further resources.

Finally, the funding provided by The Wallace Foundation was an essential ingredient for supporting cities as they developed their OST systems. Whether other cities can move forward effectively without this degree of outside support remains an open question, as does cities' ability to maintain progress in the face of an unrelenting squeeze on funding. Some cities were challenged to weave together different sources of funding while trying to build more coherent programming—a challenging task in flush times but one far more difficult in the midst of budget cuts.

While The Wallace Foundation funding pushed progress forward and the lack of it would constrain progress toward the initiative's goals, there was nothing in these case studies that indicated that progress was impossible without it. For example, the market research was not a significant expense and could be undertaken by many cities. Strong actions by mayors can lead to significant restructuring and consolidation, as was shown in Washington, D.C., and New York City. Mayors control funds that can be used to build MI systems, they can appoint special advisers, and they can demand accountability—all without adding significant financial burden.

Thus, other cities should consider what actions they can take within the confines of their specific environment. Small steps forward can add up over time to significant improvements for underserved children.

References

Banathy, Bela H., and Patrick M. Jenlink, "Systems Inquiry and Its Application in Education," in David H. Honassen, ed., *Handbook of Research on Educational Communications and Technology*, 2nd ed., Mahway, N.J.: Lawrence Erlbaum Associates, 2004, pp. 37–58.

Bodilly, Susan J., Catherine H. Augustine, and Laura Zakaras, *Revitalizing Arts Education Through Community-Wide Coordination*, Santa Monica, Calif.: RAND Corporation, MG-702-WF, 2008. As of July 20, 2010:
http://www.rand.org/pubs/monographs/MG702/

Bodilly, Susan J., and Megan K. Beckett, *Making Out-of-School-Time Matter: Evidence for an Action Agenda*, Santa Monica, Calif.: RAND Corporation, MG-242-WF, 2005. As of July 20, 2010:
http://www.rand.org/pubs/monographs/MG242/

Bodilly, Susan J., JoAn Chun, Gina Schuyler Ikemoto, and Sue Stockley, *Challenges and Potential of a Collaborative Approach to Education Reform*, Santa Monica, Calif.: RAND Corporation, MG-216-FF, 2004. As of July 20, 2010:
http://www.rand.org/pubs/monographs/MG216/

Dluhy, Milan J., *Building Coalitions in the Human Services*, Newbury Park, Calif.: Sage Publications, 1990.

Hall, Georgia, and Brooke Harvey, *Building and Sustaining Citywide Afterschool Initiatives: Experiences of the Cross-Cities Network*, Wellesley, Mass.: National Institute on Out-of-School Time, Wellesley College, 2002.

Halpern, Robert, "The Challenges of System-Building in the After-School Field," in *Critical Issues in After-School Programming*, Chicago, Ill.: Herr Research Center for Children and Social Policy, Erikson Institute, University of Chicago, 2006, pp. 77–110.

Halpern, Robert, Julie Sielberger, and Sylvan Robb, *Evaluation of the MOST (Making the Most of Out-of-School Time) Initiative: Final Report and Summary of Findings*, Chicago, Ill.: Chapin Hall Center for Children, University of Chicago, 2001.

Keith, Joanne, *Building and Maintaining Community Coalitions on Behalf of Children, Youth and Families: Community Coalitions in Action*, East Lansing, Mich.: National Network for Collaboration, 1993.

Lauer, Patricia A., Motoko Akiba, Stephanie B. Wilkerson, Helen S. Apthorp, David Snow, and Mya L. Martin-Glenn, "Out-of-School-Time Programs: A Meta-Analysis of Effects for At-Risk Students," *Review of Educational Research*, Vol. 76, No. 2, 2006, pp. 275–313.

Mattressich, Paul W., and Barbara R. Monsey, *Collaboration: What Makes It Work—A Review of Research Literature on Factors Influencing Successful Collaboration*, St. Paul, Minn.: Amherst Wilder Foundation, 1992.

McCombs, Jennifer S., Susan J. Bodilly, Nate Orr, Ethan Scherer, Louay Constant, and Daniel Gershwin, *Hours of Opportunity*, Volume 3: *Profiles of Five Cities Improving After-School Programs Through a Systems Approach*, Santa Monica, Calif.: RAND Corporation, TR-882-WF, 2010. As of September 2010: http://www.rand.org/pubs/technical_reports/TR882/

McCombs, Jennifer S., Nate Orr, Susan J. Bodilly, Scott Naftel, Louay Constant, Ethan Scherer, and Daniel Gershwin, *Hours of Opportunity*, Volume 2: *The Power of Data to Improve After-School Programs Citywide*, Santa Monica, Calif.: RAND Corporation, MG-1037/1-WF, 2010. As of September 2010: http://www.rand.org/pubs/monographs/MG1037.1/

Russell, Christina, Elizabeth R. Reisner, Lee M. Pearson, Kolajo P. Afolabi, Tiffany D. Miller, and Monica B. Mielke, *Evaluation of DYCD's Out-of-School Time Initiative; Report on the First Year*, Washington, D.C.: Policy Studies Associates, December 2006. As of July 20, 2010: http://www.policystudies.com/studies/youth/Year%201%20Final%20Report%20 12-27-06.pdf

Tushnet, Naida C., *A Guide to Developing Educational Partnerships*, Los Alamitos, Calif.: Southwest Regional Laboratory, October 1993.